Nino Rota, Federico Fellini, and the Making of an Italian Cinematic Folk Opera

NINO ROTA, FEDERICO FELLINI, AND THE MAKING OF AN ITALIAN CINEMATIC FOLK OPERA
Amarcord

Franco Sciannameo

The Edwin Mellen Press
Lewiston•Queenston•Lampeter

Library of Congress Cataloging-in-Publication Data

Sciannameo, Franco.
    Nino Rota, Federico Fellini, and the making of an Italian cinematic folk opera, Amarcord / Franco Sciannameo.
    p. cm. --
    Includes bibliographical references and index.
    Contents: From grandfather to godfather : a biographical profile of Nino Rota -- The Fellini-Rota period -- The film Amarcord -- The function of music in the film Amarcord.
    ISBN 0-7734-0808-8
    1. Rota, Nino, 1911- Amarcord. 2. Fellini, Federico. 3. Amarcord (Motion picture) 4. Motion picture music--Italy--History and criticism. I. Title: Amarcord. II. Title.

ML410.R82S35 2005
781.5'42--dc22

2005044330

hors série.

A CIP catalog record for this book is available from the British Library.

Copyright © 2005 Franco Sciannameo

All rights reserved. For information contact

    The Edwin Mellen Press   The Edwin Mellen Press
    Box 450   Box 67
    Lewiston, New York   Queenston, Ontario
    USA 14092-0450   CANADA L0S 1L0

The Edwin Mellen Press, Ltd.
Lampeter, Ceredigion, Wales
UNITED KINGDOM SA48 8LT

Printed in the United States of America

The book is dedicated to
the memory of my mother,
Noemi De Donno
(Maglie, 1916 - Bari, 2000)

TABLE OF CONTENTS

Foreword by Alan Fletcher I

Introduction and Acknowledgments V

Part One

    From Grandfather to Godfather:
    A Biographical Profile of Nino Rota 3

    The Fellini-Rota Period 19

Part Two

    The Film *Amarcord* 29

    The Function of Music in the film *Amarcord* 51

Bibliography 75

Index of Names 81

Appendix:
Campane a sera – Campane a festa 89

FOREWORD

Among the questions facing classical music today is its isolation from a mass audience. In the past century modernism, among other factors, favored a mandarin new music culture far removed from the nourishment of folk and popular sources that sustained earlier art music. Can we return to an inclusive musical culture in which leading composers write music in a variety of genres for a variety of purposes and even audiences?

Meanwhile, the past century brought to the fore a new art form in the cinema. From the beginning, the new artists of film understood that music would play a central role, but much experimentation has been undertaken to find how best to define and balance that role. Despite serious efforts from Thomson and Copland, the American film industry mostly bypassed the front ranks of its own classical composers, favoring gifted European transplants whose careers became inextricably linked with Hollywood and separated from the concert hall. Prokofiev found better luck with Eisenstein.

But lately it is observed that much of the world experiences classical music through the medium of film, and compositions like Howard Shore's *Lord of the Rings Symphony* are presented in the world's leading concert venues with great success.

The story of Nino Rota and Federico Fellini may well come to be understood as the model for the future of classical composers and their music, rather than as a glamorous anomaly. A composer trained in the most serene temples of classicized art, Rota never lost his way with a great tune or set aside his touch with a popular texture. While his muse may have become the cinema, mediated best through his thirty year association with Fellini, his oeuvre spans all forms of concert music and he remained resolutely and securely in the conservatory world.

Franco Sciannameo tells this story gracefully and with charming erudition. He weaves disparate elements of an extremely useful and evocative scenic synopsis of the music of *Amarcord*, a comprehensive bibliography, a profile of the composer, a table of Rota's works throughout the Fellini period, and even a lagniappe of some delightful but previously unknown bell music by Rota, connecting all by means of a discerning investigation of how Rota and Fellini together found an ideal synthesis of music and film, seen through the lens of one of their greatest collaborations, *Amarcord*. Sciannameo's translation of Fellini's eulogy to Rota is a particularly touching, and telling, inclusion.

Fellini's films and Rota's music have certainly become part of a global currency of cultural meaning and in that sense require no explanation or special pleading. But it is exceptionally interesting and useful to have Sciannameo's notes on the songs and sources for musical material, tracing particular meanings both personal and political. The 'found music' employed and transformed by Rota often has many layers of intention and Sciannameo is superb in finding and explaining these "sounds and melodies embedded with communal values."

Along the way we encounter everyone from Attali and Adorno, Barthes and Benjamin through Zarlino. Probably no discussion of *Amarcord* could be without Sciannameo's apposite and delicate reference to Proust; we also learn from discourses on Brueghel, Manet, Baudelaire, and a whole tapestry of cultural context. The central concept introduced in the title – Rota's embodiment of the tradition of folk opera in Fellini's films – is persuasive and highly suggestive. It spans the work of Strauss in bringing an essentially vernacular dance music into the grand opera and the movement of Weill into the cabaret. The idea that montage can underlie a new concept of musical form, in Sciannameo's words "thematic leitmotifs which are structured mosaically," is fruitful in consideration of music as diverse as Stravinsky and Marshall Mathers. The lover of music will find much to think about in this monograph and the lover of film will be delighted throughout. In presenting what Fellini called "the miracles of Nino Rota," Sciannameo succeeds in conveying a deep feeling of tenderness as well.

Alan Fletcher
Professor and Head
School of Music
Carnegie Mellon University
Pittsburgh, Pennsylvania
February 2005

INTRODUCTION AND ACKNOWLEDGMENTS

This study presents functional and cultural analyses of the music Nino Rota used to underscore Federico Fellini's film *Amarcord*.

Aside from three main original compositions, Rota incorporated an array of popular and patriotic music fashionable in Italy in the 1930's. Seldom in the history of film music has such a task been accomplished with more taste and perspicacity.

Fellini's film is about "remembering" episodes which occurred during his youth in the town of Rimini on the Northern Adriatic coast of Italy. Nino Rota spent the 1940's and 1950's in Torre a Mare a resort town eleven kilometers south of Bari, along the Adriatic Sea. Consequently, the two artists shared the experience of a Mediterranean way of life. Torre a Mare is also my Italian home. It was there, in the post World War II years, that I spent my boyhood and many summers thereafter.

At that time I was too young to remember Rota or the sound of his piano. As a musician, I met him many years later in Rome during the synchronization of some of his film music. I remember how satisfactory those recording sessions were and how pleasant it was to see a famous composer marvel as his own music came to life. The studio suddenly became a jovial, relaxed place, a rare instance in a professional environment controlled by the rigor of the stopwatch. I saw Rota again at the *Accademia Nazionale di Santa Cecilia*, coming on stage to acknowledge a standing ovation after the Roman première of his *Mysterium*. I was a member of the orchestra and proud of him.

Many of the situations and characters in *Amarcord* bear remarkable similarity to daily life in Torre a Mare and vicinity. Thus, Rota's musical contribution to the film becomes a poetical evocation of Fellini's, and Rota's own *Lieux de Mémoire*, echoing Proust's assertion that writing about art is nothing but a process of recalling one's childhood. Furthermore, if one thinks that the music identifies the characters in this film as "a people," the music, then, can be considered an abstract representation of their social organization -- familiar sounds and melodies embedded with communal values. As Simon Frith observed, "Music constructs our sense of identity through the experiences it offers of the body, time, and sociability, experiences which enable us to place ourselves in imaginative cultural narratives."[1]

This study does not contain a complete examination of the Fellini-Rota collaboration. Such a project would have been a redundancy, since several films have been discussed separately by various critics (see Bibliography). I have chosen to focus on the film *Amarcord* for two reasons. First, in my view, it represents the two artists' collaboration more fully than any other. Secondly, because in *Amarcord* Nino Rota and Federico Fellini have combined, consciously or not, elements common to a folk-opera, i.e. stories or episodes drawn from a people's culture with song and dance typical to their everyday life. In this the stories are colored by sometimes elegant, sometimes earthy, sometimes surreal, popular overtones.

I will examine *Amarcord* as a musical work -- an Italian cinematic folk-opera. What I call "cinematic folk-opera" emerged in the late 1950's, filtered through both operatic *verismo* and cinematic *neorealismo*. It served to re-channel the cultural migration of Italian mass audiences from the opera house to the movie theatre. Once the Italians reached the conclusion that contemporary opera was no longer endowed with memorable arias -- the traditional supporting pillars of the operatic edifice -- audiences shifted their attention to cinema, favoring those productions featuring "singable" characters and situations (including a cornucopia of operas on film). Those who composed music for the cinema were, then, particularly aware that those films were going to be regarded for decades to come

---

[1] Frith, Simon. *Performing Rites: On the Value of Popular Music* (Cambridge, MA: Harvard University Press, 1996): 269.

as their "operas." Nino Rota (1911-1979) and Ennio Morricone (1928-) reached great success with the masses by enhancing their film scores with arias/tunes/songs of extraordinary vocal expressiveness, thus satisfying the Italian audiences' longing for operatic *bel canto*.

A number of these films, beginning with the very colorful *Carosello napoletano* (1954) by Ettore Giannini, scored by Raffaele Gervasio, constitute a corpus of works which fit, in a Gramscian sense, the Italian cinematic folk-opera category.[2] By applying the same methodology, *Amarcord* becomes a prime example of Italian cinematic folk-opera set in Mussolini's time.

It seems that every country possesses some sort of national opera, a *Gesamkunstwerk* reflecting the idiom and idiosyncrasies of a particular people, embedded in a music they could have invented and performed themselves. Strange as it seems, Italy really has no national opera. Puccini's operas, *La boheme, Manon Lescaut, Tabarro,* and *La rondine* are based on French stories; *Madama Butterfly, La fanciulla del West* and *Turandot* were inspired by the Far East and the American West. Only *Tosca, Suor Angelica,* and *Gianni Schicchi* have an Italian background. Indeed, the rhythms of a *tarantella* evoke the notions of *sole e amore*, quickly available in the Bay of Naples, but little else. And yes, there is perhaps more Sicilian folklore in the film *The Godfather* than in *Cavalleria rusticana*, notwithstanding Francis Ford Coppola's fusion of the two in the final scene of *The Godfather, Part III.* If anything, one may think of local, regional folklore, but not of a true national folkloric synthesis. After all, the cultures of Alpine (Northern) Italy, and Mediterranean (Southern) Italy have very little in common -- a problem of national identity that was particularly acute during the xenophobic Fascist period.

Benito Mussolini, a sensitive music listener, longed for a type of opera which could fully express the concept of Italianicity according to Fascist ideology. The closest specimens to the dictatorial quest was Franco Alfano's *La leggenda di Sakuntala*, the unlikely story of an Indian Princess, Mascagni's

---

[2] Gramsci, Antonio. *Selections from the Cultural Writings.* David Forgacs, ed. (Cambridge, MA: Harvard University Press, 1985).

dreadful *Nerone*, or Malipiero's operas about the origins of Venice. In the end, the dream was abandoned as scores drenched in trite *verismo* began to flood *Il Duce*'s desk.

The truth was that Mussolini himself had become the quintessential Italian folk-hero/folk-villain: somebody to worship and/or spit upon, the demiurgic representative of a secular religion sanctioned by the Catholic Church, in the pursuit of total control over the Italian people.

Fellini's *Amarcord* is perhaps the best and most human portraiture of Mussolini's Italy, the *italietta*, the provincial Italy of the folks whose consensus Mussolini craved so much. From this point of view, *Amarcord* is like a garland of Italian folk-tales carved in the Calvino's tradition and strung together by the music of Nino Rota.

This book is organized into two parts. Part One provides a biographical profile of Rota, my translation of Fellini's *L'amico magico* (see pages 13-17), and a comparative table showing Rota's creative activities from 1952 to 1979 *vis-à-vis* Fellini's films. Part Two offers annotated critical accounts of *Amarcord* from 1973 to present, and the various interpretations of the characters and stories portrayed in it. Finally, I analyze the function of Rota's music in the cultural context that prompted the composer's and the director's choice of material.

A bibliography, dealing with Rota, Fellini, and film music in general, concludes the volume's second part. In the appendix, I offer two rare brief compositions by Nino Rota *Campane a sera* and *Campane a festa*, both written during his student days at Curtis. These pieces, intended to be played on the carillon, reveal a quintessential Rota with all his candor and simplicity.

I wish to thank Nina Rota, the composer's daughter, for sharing with me memories of her father; Professor Franco Giannelli, a long-time friend from Torre a Mare who knew Rota intimately, for his many Rota anecdotes; Professor Dinko Fabris, of the *Conservatorio "Niccoló Piccinni"* in Bari, for his scholarly understanding of Rota's *modus operandi*; and Maestro Nicola Scardicchio, professor of composition at the *Conservatorio* and Rota's pupil for his help and encouragement.

I wish to extend special thanks to friends and colleagues Paul Chihara of the University of California at Los Angeles and Marcia Landy of the University of Pittsburgh for their interest in my research and their critical reading of earlier drafts of these pages. I express my gratitude to Peter Bondanella of Indiana University for kindly providing me with copy of *Amarcord*'s English subtitles and Hollywood composer/historian Jeannie Pool for publishing my earlier sketch of Nino Rota's biography in *The Cue Sheet*.

Particular thanks go to my sister, Luciana Sciannameo, for her love and enthusiasm concerning Italy's fading traditions and for accompanying me on many "field trips."

Finally, I wish to express a special thanks to my wife, Louise Sciannameo, for her editorial acumen and love.

Franco Sciannameo
Distinguished Scholar in Multidisciplinary Studies
School of Music
Carnegie Mellon University
Pittsburgh, Pennsylvania
February 2005

PART ONE

FROM GRANDFATHER TO GODFATHER:
A BIOGRAPHICAL PROFILE OF NINO ROTA
The ephemeral, the contingent, and the consequential

Twentieth century Italian music is a complex maze of styles, currents, and counter-currents characterized by the emergence of sporadic original voices. Nino Rota's was amongst such voices. In fact, one does not discuss Rota in the same breath as the controversial Giacinto Scelsi or Goffredo Petrassi and Luigi Dallapiccola, his most illustrious, "consequential" contemporaries with whom he shared friendship and esteem.

Critics' attempts to evaluate Rota's *œuvre* show their sincere affection and appreciation for the musician and his music. Their writings, though, are often veiled by a sort of frustration as Rota's "music without a crisis" eludes their exegesis. The matter becomes more complex when critics make further efforts to establish significant distinctions between the composer's "serious" music and his film scores. There is no clear differentiation here. Paraphrasing Baudelaire's definition of modernity as ephemeral, fugitive, and contingent, I can say that the consequentiality of Rota's music is to be found in its postmodern ephemerality.

Nino Rota made a good living as a composer. At no time was he distracted by the intricate politics infesting the Italian cultural spectrum. He survived Italian Fascism, the war, the growing pains of the Italian Republic, and its scandalous plunge into corruption. Can he be faulted for having been politically skeptical – despite his position as the director of a state conservatory? Many critics have accused him of having been an opportunistic crowd pleaser, a *retro* paying token homage to modernity, a sold-out tunesmith serving the capitalistic international film industry. I prefer to envision Rota as a "displaced" 19th-century Italian opera composer, a "prolific rabbit" as Heine called Donizetti, writing music on demand whose *raison d'écrire* was not the opera house but, rather the 20th-century's only original art form: cinema.

Nino Rota was born in Milan on December 3, 1911. His maternal grandfather was Giovanni Rinaldi (1840-1895).[1]

At the age of four Rota played the piano well, having been initiated to the keyboard by his mother, Ernesta (1880-1945), who remained his piano teacher, friend, and confidante.[2] It seems, at some point, that Rota also took piano lessons from Giovanni Maria Anfossi (1864-1946), a famous Milanese pedagogue.[3]

When he was eight, Rota composed some songs for voice and piano dedicated to his father's cousin, Anna Maria Rota, a noted vocalist, and *Storia del mago doppio*, a prelude and fugue for piano four-hands written to serve as a commentary to a fable of his own invention. What foreshadowing for the adult composer who ultimately made film music his specialty!

Giacomo Orefice (1865-1922), professor of composition at the Milan Conservatory, showed interest in the eight-year-old composer and accepted him as an auditor in his composition class. During this period Rota also studied with Giovanni Perlasca, Giulio Bas, and Paolo Delachi. At age eleven, Rota completed the score of the oratorio *L'infanzia di San Giovanni* for vocal soloists, chorus and orchestra, performed first in Milan on April 22, 1923 and then in Turcoing, France to great acclaim. He was hailed by the international press as the "new

---

[1] Giovanni Rinaldi was one among the few 19th-century Italian composers who wrote only piano music. Although such a cultural undercurrent in a country dominated by the complex world of opera has been historically epitomized by the figures of Giovanni Sgambati (1841-1914) and Giuseppe Martucci (1856-1909), Giovanni Rinaldi could rightfully join them. He wrote hundreds of short pieces which stylistically echoed Chopin, Schumann, Scriabin, and Debussy, while always preserving an Italianate connotation and a great deal of originality. The validity of Rinaldi's music has been pointed out from time to time. In 1941, Lidia Carbonatto presented a thesis at the Facoltà di Lettere-Universitá di Torino entitled *Giovanni Rinaldi, pianista, didatta e compositore*, and "Giovanni Rinaldi, un precursore dell'impressionismo musicale," *La Rassegna Musicale*, 1941: 453-62. Manlio La Morgia published a short but eloquent essay, "Giovanni Rinaldi: indicazioni per lo studio di un musicista da 'riscoprire,'in *I grandi anniversary del 1960* (Siena:Accademia Musicale Chigiana, MCMLX): 200-220. Nino Rota himself was very enthusiastic about his grandfather's music, as he stated on many occasions. At the dawn of his career he even signed his name as Nino Rota-Rinaldi, Nino being a diminutive of Giovanni.

[2] See Ernesta Rota-Rinaldi. *Mio padre e storia di Nino*, a cura di Francesco Lombardi. Comune di Reggiolo (Reggiolo, 1999).

[3] Anfossi, the teacher of famous pianist Arturo Benedetti Michelangeli, also taught Luisa Báccara (1892-1985), a fine pianist and Gabriele D'Annunzio's companion and music consultant. Nino Rota was one of the very few friends who visited this lady on a regular basis. Following D'Annunzio's death in 1937, she became a recluse. Rota and Báccara shared, among other things, memories of Anfossi, their piano teacher. See Antonella Federici. *Luisa Báccara* (Venezia: Neri Pozza, 1994): 15.

Mozart," and news of the event even reached the pages of *The New York Times* (October 21, 1923).

From 1924 to 1926, Rota studied composition privately with Ildebrando Pizzetti (1880-1968), who was then director of the Milan Conservatory. During this period the adolescent musician composed his first opera, *Il principe porcaro (The Swineherd Prince)*, after Hans Christian Andersen, and a *Concerto* for cello and orchestra (1925).[4] Following a disagreement with Pizzetti, who wished his pupil, and probably Signora Rota, to refrain from having Nino's student works publicly performed and, above all, published, the Rotas sought new teachers. At first they thought of Charles Koechlin (1867-1950), but then the choice became Maurice Ravel (1875-1937), who, at that time, was on a concert tour of Italy.[5] After having attentively examined Nino's works and complimenting the boy, Ravel decided not to take him on as a pupil.[6] In the meantime, Rota kept his pen moving under the tutelage of Mario Castelnuovo-Tedesco (1895-1968).[7]

In 1927, the composer moved to Rome to study with Alfredo Casella (1883-1947). The most progressive Italian musician of the period, Casella made sure Rota was exposed to new musical trends. From Rome, Casella maintained contact with the most important musicians in the world, allowing Rota many opportunities to meet the finest composers, from Manuel De Falla to Igor Stravinsky. With the latter Rota began a friendship which lasted a lifetime.[8]

---

[4] *Il principe porcaro*'s orchestration was never finished, so the opera remained unperformed until September 27, 2003 when a new version, prepared by Nicola Scardicchio, was presented at the *Teatro Goldoni* in Venice.
[5] In the course of a radio interview entitled *Voi ed io* (RAI, 1978), Rota offered a vivid account of his meeting with Maurice Ravel. Apparently, the teenaged Rota was not too impressed by Ravel's statement that in order to be a good composer one should master, as a pianist, the works of Chopin and Liszt especially since he [Ravel] was, according to Rota, a pianist of modest means. See Ermanno Comuzio and Paolo Vecchi. *138 1/2: i film di Nino Rota* (Reggio Emilia: Assessorato alla Cultura, 1987): 16.
[6] Ravel acted more or less in the same fashion with George Gershwin (1898-1937), when the American composer wished to study with him in Paris. See David Ewen. *George Gershwin: His Journey to Greatness* (New York: The Ungar Publishing Co., 1976. 2nd 1986): 132.
[7] Rota and Castelnuovo-Tedesco kept in touch until Mario Castelnuovo-Tedesco's death in 1968. The latter told this writer during a conversation in Beverly Hills (March 1964), that Rota always sent him a *panettone* from Italy at Christmas time, a gesture which, aside from the customary exchange of letters and postcards, was particularly dear to him.
[8] Rota was close to Stravinsky from the time of their first meeting in Rome in the late 1920' when the young composer accompanied Stravinsky on a concert tour of France and Spain.

In 1930, after three years of intense study, Rota took the Diploma in Composition examination at the "Santa Cecilia" Conservatory in Rome: Casella insisted that the young composer have his "papers" in order. Moreover, after private tutoring with Michele Cianciulli,[9] Rota embarked upon obtaining a baccalaureate and a university degree as well. In 1937, the composer earned a degree in the Humanities from the University of Milan. Appropriately for a musician, Rota presented a thesis on Gioseffo Zarlino.[10] Thereafter, Arturo Toscanini, a long-time friend of Giovanni Rinaldi and the Rota family, suggested that Rota go to Philadelphia to study at The Curtis Institute of Music.[11] 1931 and 1932 were spent at Curtis. Rota studied composition with Rosario Scalero and conducting with Fritz Reiner.[12] It seems that Toscanini disliked the fact that, in Rome, Rota was under what he described as Casella's "arid and cerebral" influence.[13] At Curtis, Rota had among his classmates Samuel Barber (1910-1981) and Giancarlo Menotti (1911-); he also began a friendship with Aaron Copland. Young Rota, Barber and Menotti, were invited to contribute some short works for the Curtis Carillon Series published by Schirmer in 1934. Rota's contributing pieces were entitled *Campane a sera* and *Campane a festa*. (See Appendix).

When Rota returned to Italy from America, he was already a mature composer equipped with an unusually eclectic musical background, including much Cole Porter, Gershwin, Irving Berlin and Copland. In Italy, he probed the fields of popular music, commercial song and operetta, absorbing styles and

---

[9] Rota became particularly attached to Professor Cianciulli who was also responsible for introducing the musician to esoteric studies, a passion Rota cultivated for the rest of his life.
[10] The title of Rota's thesis was "Aspetti tecnici ed estetici della musica nel Rinascimento visti attraverso la teoria di Giuseffo Zarlino."
[11] Toscanini had made a similar suggestion to the Menotti family; in fact, Giancarlo entered Curtis in the fall of 1928. See John Gruen. *Menotti: A Biography* (New York: McMillan Publishing Co., Inc. 1978): 16.
[12] Rosario Scalero (Torino, 1870-1945) was a virtuoso violinist who studied with Camillo Sivori, the only pupil of Paganini, and August Wilhelmj. He was also a composer of renown; he studied composition in Vienna with Eusebius Mandyczewski who was a friend of Johannes Brahms. Many of Scalero's works were published by Breitkopf unde Hartel. In 1919, Scalero came to the United States to head the composition department at the Mannes School of Music in New York. In 1928, he was appointed to Curtis. This singular musician was the teacher of Barber, Menotti, Rota, Foss, Rorem and many more important composers.
[13] See José Maria Latorre. *Nino Rota, La imagen de la Musica* (Barcellona: Montesinos, 1987): 30.

idioms which soon were put to good use. In 1933, he had an opportunity to write his first soundtrack for a film by debutante director Raffaello Matarazzo (1909-1966).

Treno popolare, presented a series of entertaining episodes aboard a train carrying members of the Italian working class on a short, state-sponsored vacation trip in the countryside. The film reflected a key element in Mussolini's plan to gain consensus by evolving a kind of mass, lowbrow culture based on standardized forms of leisure and diversion rather than intellectual involvement.[14]

The soundtrack of this first film consisted of facile songs and little marches written in a style very much in tune with the political and social climate of the time portrayed in the film. Some of these tunes, once published "in folio" and recorded, had a successful life of their own, making Rota a popular name almost overnight, an unusual achievement for a young, "classically" trained composer.[15] The film *per se*, however, was a flop and Rota's debut in film music seemed truncated at the start, much to the relief of his "classical" supporters. As a sort of compromise Rota tried his hand at incidental music. This time it was a humorous work by Sergio Tofano entitled *Bonaventura nell'isola dei pappagalli* which was staged in 1936. During the same period Rota composed a remarkable Sonata for viola and piano (1934-35), a much performed Sonata for violin and piano (1936-37),[16] an engaging Quintetto for flute, oboe, viola, cello, and harp (1935), a delicate Sonata for flute and harp (1937)[17] and his Sinfonia No. 1 (1935-39) dedicated to Goffredo Petrassi.

These compositions, which constitute the best of Nino Rota's post-Curtis period, reflect the influences of Pizzetti, Casella, and, above all, Gian Francesco Malipiero (1882-1973). They were all published by Ricordi, with the exception of

---

[14] For important views on Italian cinema of this period see Marcia Landy. *Fascism in Film: The Italian Commercial Cinema, 1931-1943* (Princeton, NJ: Princeton University Press, 1986) and James Hay. *Popular Film Culture in Fascist Italy: The Passing of the Rex* (Bloomingotn, IN: Indiana University Press, 1987).

[15] The fox-trot *Treno popolare* (lyrics by Ennio Neri) was released on a 78 rpm disc (Columbia DQ 622), while the sheet music was published by Edizioni Musicali Pittaluga in Torino.

[16] Often performed by Luigi Dallapiccola in duo with violinist Sandro Materassi.

[17] Also available in a version for ten instruments published by Ricordi under the title *Sonata da Camera*.

the Sonata for viola and piano published as late as 1998 by Schott Musik International.[18]

Aside from his exploits as an *enfant-prodige*, Rota was established as a composer at home in both "classical" and "popular" genres, a situation which, although favorable, became a stigma for the rest of his career – and after. In 1937, Rota entered a new phase of activity: teaching. He was, in fact, appointed to teach just about everything at the *Liceo Musicale* in Taranto, the ancient city of *Tarentum* on the Ionian Sea in Southern Italy, perhaps historically important but certainly not in the mainstream of musical events. According to Rota himself, the two Taranto years (1937-38) were a miserable experience during which he almost ceased composing. Soon, however, Rota was in Bari, an important city on the Southern Adriatic shore, as professor of harmony and counterpoint at the local *Liceo Musicale*. This happened in 1939. Ten years later, Nino Rota became the much loved director of that institution which, in 1959, was elevated to the rank of State Conservatory, the *Conservatorio "Niccolò Piccinni."* Rota kept both the Bari position and his residence until retirement in 1977.[19]

Cinema made a call to Rota again in 1942 with another film by Matarazzo. The new film was titled *Giorno di nozze*, a lovely comedy much enhanced by Rota's songs. It was a decent box office success and solidified his presence in film music for a lifetime. He was thirty-one-years-old.

Throughout the 1940's, Nino Rota worked as principal composer for Lux Film, a cinematic enterprise administered by Guido M. Gatti and directed by Fedele D'Amico who were also preeminent figures in Italian music and the

---

[18] Interesting comments on Rota's early works can be found in Giannandrea Gavazzeni's "Brevi capitoli su Nino Rota" in *Musicisti d'Europa. Studi sui contemporanei* (Milano: Suvini-Zerboni, 1955): 266-296.
[19] The city and the people of both Bari and Torre a Mare have paid homage to their honorary citizen. Symposia and concerts are periodically organized in honor of the musician who has been immortalized in streets and buildings named after him. See Dinko Fabris (ed.) *Nino Rota compositore del nostro tempo* (Bari: Orchestra Sinfonica di Bari, 1987) and *La Musica a Bari*, edited by Dinko Fabris and Marco Renzi (Bari: Levante Editori, 1993). The latter book expands considerably on Rota's activity at the Conservatorio and in Bari generally.

authors of essays promoting Italian contemporary composers.[20] It was certainly by no mere chance that Gatti and D'Amico selected Rota as chief staff composer at Lux. His first assignment was a film by Renato Castellani, *Zazá* (1942), an important picture for which Rota composed a dense score, including a dozen songs portraying the nostalgic, decadent turn-of-the-century world. The ending of the picture substantially reflected the connotations of the operatic *verismo* of Mascagni and Giordano. In 1950, the composer began an important collaboration with Eduardo De Filippo (1900-1984), the great Neapolitan actor and playwright. He and Federico Fellini ultimately became the two main pillars of Rota's fame and career. In the meantime, the musician conquered the operatic stage by presenting, in April 1955, at the Teatro Massimo in Palermo, *Il cappello di paglia di Firenze*. The immediate appeal of this opera, based on Eugene Labiche's play, was reconfirmed by a memorable production at the *Piccola Scala* in Milan under the direction of Giorgio Strehler. The year was 1958. The opera made the rounds of the major opera houses and the success of Rota's music was something of a shock to the Italian critics of the Left who wished to relegate Rota to film scoring. They had thought that with this opera Rota was thumbing his nose at "serious music." Instead, though, the musician proved to be extremely organic and faithful to his artistic *credo* by fusing much of his film music into his opera which was even termed as a masterpiece.

There is a certain amount of critical literature about *Il cappello di paglia di Firenze* which generated something of a polemic between liberal critics of the Left and the conservatives. An abstract from a review written by Franco Chieco in 1965, a time when conservatism in Italy was often viewed as a euphemism for dilettantism, stated: "It is true that Nino Rota has a precise personality, singular not only artistically but from a human standpoint as well. Perhaps it is a mistake to make him appear extraneous to the problems of our age. If anything, he is a fortunate man: he nourishes himself with optimism. Why, then should he not nourish music with optimism? *Il cappello di paglia di Firenze* is the happiest

---

[20] For details on this important studio, see Alberto Farassino and Tatti Sanguinetti. *Lux Film: Esthétique et systéme d'un studio italien* (Locarno: Editions du Festival International du Film de Locarno, 1984) and Alberto Farassino. *Lux Film* (Milano: Il Castoro, 2000).

product of his creative season. An opera written with a smile. A game which seems to mock the very same cheerfulness of the farcical subject, but with much gracefulness, refinement, and sense of humor filtered through Rota's impeccable taste. The four *tableaux* comprising the opera run smoothly in a succession of refreshingly sightful arias, splendid *concertati*, spicy and dynamic recitatives woven in a pleasant, graceful and vivaciously comic musical context. This music is always ready to echo or parody 18th-century *opera buffa*, Viennese operetta, and Parisian *vaudeville*. It is the unmistakable product of Rota's ingenuous and masterful assimilation."

Nino Rota spent the 1940's and 1950's in Torre a Mare, then a fishing village eleven kilometers south of Bari along the Adriatic Sea. There, away from Rome and the vortex of Cinecittá where "everybody wanted Nino," Rota felt "in total control of himself and his time," and concerning film music, he wrote to his cousin Titina Rota, " if it was not for my usual fear that by rejecting a film offer it won't come back when needed, I'd throw the whole business out of the window."[21]

Prior to *Il cappello di paglia di Firenze*, the musician wrote two operas of large proportion: *Ariodante* (1938-41) and *Torquemada* (1943), strange dramatic works composed in 19th-Century Italian operatic style. *Ariodante* was premiered in Parma on November 22, 1942 as part of the festival *Teatro delle Novitá di Bergamo*, before a cheerful audience and dismayed critics. *Torquemada* was never performed. During this period, Rota compose several other works including an outstanding Concerto for harp and orchestra (1943), *Sinfonia sopra una canzone d'amore* (1947), *Variazioni sopra un tema gioviale for orchestra* (1953), the chamber opera *I due timidi* (1950), and another Sonata for viola (or clarinet) and piano (1945). These compositions were all published by Ricordi. The Harp Concerto received many performances by the artist to whom the work was dedicated, Clelia Gatti Aldrovanti. She also recorded it.[22] *Variazioni sopra un tema gioviale* have been in the repertoire of major orchestras. The chamber opera,

---

[21] See Francesco Lombardi. *Fra cinema e musica del Novecento: Il caso Nino Rota dai documenti* (ANR-Studi II, 2000) (Firenze: Leo S. Olschki, 2000): 37.
[22] Salvi Label NSM 1/2. Carlo Maria Giulini, Conducting. [Original 1948 performance]

I due timidi, written originally as a radio opera to a story by Suso Cecchi D'Amico, became successful also as a staged performance. The *Sinfonia sopra una canzone d'amore*, although completed in 1947, was not performed and published until 1972. Three movements of this work, however, were already well-known. Rota had used this material for the soundtracks of the motion pictures *The Glass Mountain* (Henry Cass, 1949) and *Il Gattopardo* (Luchino Visconti, 1963). Moreover, the "tema d'amore" upon which the Sinfonia is based was taken from the score composed for another film, *La donna della montagna* (Renato Castellani, 1943). This is a prime example of Rota's eclecticism and his refusal to make hierarchical distinctions between film music and "serious" music.

Fellini made his debut as film director "in toto" in 1952. The movie was *Lo sceicco bianco* starring Alberto Sordi. Fellini asked Rota to score the soundtrack, the two men met and Rota "reluctantly" (his word) accepted the offer. Thus, the great collaboration began; it lasted for three decades.

When Fellini first approached Rota, the musician was already a celebrity in his field and a very busy man at that, while the director was on his first "solo flight." Rota is now mostly remembered for having been Fellini's musician, though at that time, Fellini was the little-known artist.

The Fellini-Rota string of successes did not prevent the musician from achieving other impressive musical goals, not only with his composition of numerous concert works but also in collaboration with other film directors: Luchino Visconti (*Il Gattopardo*, 1963) and Franco Zeffirelli (*La bisbetica domata*, 1967 and *Romeo e Giulietta*, 1968), among others. Another milestone of the 1960's was Rota's collaboration with Rita Wertmüller, culminating in *Il giornalino di Gian Burrasca*, a 1965 eleven-part television series.[23] Rota composed some 50 songs for this production some of which, like *La pappa col pomodoro*, became extremely popular jingles among youngsters and adults alike. Rota's critics were more outraged than ever; some said the composer had fallen to the lowest degree of any artistic and ethical decency, especially in light of his

---

[23] Interestingly, *Gian Burrasca* was revived in 2002 by Italian television, showcasing a new cast and state-of-the-art technologies while preserving Rota's original music.

position as the director of a major musical institution. In reality, what the critics failed to appreciate was that Rota, a famous composer and educator, had dared to write a silly, because it was appropriately so, tune for the most popular and infamous medium of the turbulent 1960's – television – while harvesting success after success in cinema, opera and the concert hall without ever changing his stylistic personality.[24]

By the time Rota completed the music for Fellini's *Il Casanova* in 1976, he had already received an Oscar for the soundtrack of *The Godfather* (Part II) and staged the premiere of his last major opera, *Napoli milionaria*, based on a play by Eduardo De Filippo.

This opera, first performed at the *Teatro Nuovo* in Spoleto on June 22, 1977, represents another synthesis of Rota's stylistic eclecticism. It includes material from film scores *Napoli milionaria, Filumena Marturano, Le notti di Cabiria, Plein Soleil, La dolce vita, Rocco e i suoi fratelli, Le tentazioni del dottor Antonio, Toby Dammit,* and *Waterloo*.

Upon release of *The Godfather* (Part I) and the enormous commercial success of its "love theme," Rota was accused of plagiarism. The maestro paid no attention to such a fracas because he was well aware of the tune's origin. It first appeared in the film *Fortunella* for which he had composed the soundtrack in 1958. If anything, it was a case of self-plagiarism. The situation, however, became aggravated by the intervention of *Fortunella*'s producer Dino De Laurentis who demanded his rights to the tune, although, it was discovered, he had never paid Rota a cent for the work done on the film in the first place. The case, although officially closed, provoked a number of Italian film music composers, siding with De Laurentis, to send a telegram of protest to the American Academy Awards Committee upon hearing of Rota's nomination for an Oscar. The committee withdrew the nomination and Rota had to wait for *The Godfather* (Part II) to collect his long due award, which he shared with Carmine Coppola, Francis Ford's father.

---

[24] Italian television music has always been much influenced by Hollywood. Rota and later Ennio Morricone were the only Italian composers of talent who viewed the medium as an opportunity for innovative musical ideas.

Rota died on April 10, 1979. He was an "authentic" and deserving musician of our time, a musician for whom there existed no barriers of genres, categories, or qualifications. For Rota, music was just music or, as Fellini would have put it, Nino was music, like the jongleur of old. Nino Rota's life was dedicated to his music, the Conservatory, and an unusual group of friends. Rota's companion and confidante had always been Ernesta, his mother. Upon her death, the composer lived alone in a large apartment in old Papal Rome and in one-room studio at the Conservatory in Bari. He also had a major interest in hermeticism, a passion he shared with a select group of intellectuals headed by Vinci Verginelli (19031987), the author of many texts, which Rota set to music. Rota e Verginelli researched and collected a priceless library of rare hermetic texts dating from the 15th, 16th, 17th and 18th centuries. The collection, comparable in size and quality to the Paul and Mary Mellon Collection (Alchemy and the Occult) at Yale University, filled the rooms of Rota's house in Rome. Upon Verginelli's death in 1987 the collection was given to the *Accademia dei Lincei* in Rome.[25]

The rest of Rota's personal papers are now preserved at the *Archivio Nino Rota* (ANR) housed at *Fondazione Giorgio Cini* in Venice.

Nino Rota's interest in hermetic matters is revelatory for future studies concerning this musician's thinking, personality, his views of the world, and the people around him. Even Federico Fellini, despite thirty years of collaboration, was not part of Rota's "inner circle." Professional life was, then, rigorously separated from personal goals. In fact, in writing Rota's eulogy, Fellini revealed that at times, he felt puzzled by certain aspects of Rota's behavior; Fellini's exquisite sensitivity detected something extraordinary in Rota but could not quite put a finger on it. Here is how, having to deliver Rota's eulogy, he defined his friend simply as magical: " I would have preferred to speak about Nino Rota in the course of a less sad occasion, without the uncomfortable feelings generated by the idea that he is no more, deep feelings of tenderness which his departure have

---

[25] *Bibliotheca Hermetica. Catalogo alqaunto ragionato della Raccolta Verginelli-Rota di Antichi Testi Ermetici (secoli XV-XVIII)*, (Firenze: Nardini Editore, 1986).

awakened in myself and in all those who have known him, as a musician and as a man.

It may seem hard to believe but it is a really difficult to remember when I met him. It could appear rhetorical but I had the impression I had known him forever. Ours was not a relationship like any other, a relationship that develops, grows, decreases. It was a relationship which never changed. The first time we looked each other in the eye, we had the sensation of having found each other again and we went side by side. Everything happened during that moment. I used to see him often at the Lux Studios in *Via Po*; I saw that little man, defenseless, kind, always smiling, always looking for doors which did not exist to make an exit; he could have made an exit through a window like a butterfly wrapped up in a magical, unreal cloud. What was most fascinating about him was his availability and, at the same time, his total absence. In any place or on occasion or for any reason, when you met him, he always gave you the impression that it was by chance, but at the same time he gave you the assurance that you could count on him, that he could accompany you for awhile. That was exactly what happened between us. We met at the Lux entryway and, because I was leaving, he walked with me for a long stretch. We walked along the entire Via Po. When we stopped at a traffic light and I was about to say goodbye I asked him, "Where are you going?" He replied, "I was going to the Lux Studios, I must go to Lux." Yet, through the indeterminate nature of his relationships, his way of appearing and disappearing, his elusiveness, giving the impression of a child crossing the *Via del Tritone* in the most chaotic moment of traffic, he was the most punctual, precise, and available man one could think of. He was "helped" by something invisible; he went through risky situations carelessly, as though he were protected by a magic wrapper, by an invisible diaphragm. I don't think that Nino Rota ever experienced a mishap, although he did not wear a watch and had a vague notion of the day and month he was in. He believed that the 20th hours was 10 p.m., and one day, when he had to fly to Zurich at 8 p.m., he went to the airport at 21:15 convinced he had time to spare for cappuccino and newspapers. At 10 p.m. (22nd hour) he went to the information desk to check if there was a delay. "The 20:00 plane has already taken off sir," said the clerk, "perfectly on time." Rota replied, "But it is barely ten o'clock (22:00)." "Exactly," replied the clerk, a little alarmed. This is the only instance I know in which reality had the best of him, otherwise never a mishap. At appointments, he always arrived at the last moments, but he arrived! The kind of magic atmosphere he generated around himself gave the impression that something prodigious was going to happen, and he was able to communicate such a feeling to others. When he was about, you knew that it was going to be all right. Nino was a person carrying a rare gift that belonged to the sphere of intuition. Such was the gift that kept him so innocent, graceful, happy. I don't wish to be misunderstood here. He was not a kind of wizard. On the contrary. Often he made very sharp observations, offering opinions on people and facts with impressive precision. Like children, like simple-minded people, like certain sensitive persons, like certain innocent and candid people, all of a sudden he said dazzling things. Between us there was an immediate understanding, full, total since our first film *Lo sceicco bianco*. When I decided to become a full time film director, Nino was already there beforehand like a premonition. Nino had no need to see my films; in fact, he often fell deeply asleep during showings, then suddenly watched the screen and said, "How beautiful that tree is!" Of course he had to watch the films a dozen times at the editing machine in order to establish the timing of his music and yet, it was like he was not watching them at all. He had a geometric imagination, a celestial vision of music; therefore, the images in my films did not concern him much. He lived in an internal world in which reality had no access. At the same time he was a great musician, a great orchestrator, and a great organizer; his scoring was just perfect.

I used to sit next to him on the piano bench, narrating the film, explaining the meaning I wished to convey through the images of each sequence and the type of music I wanted to accompany them. But Nino was not following me; he was distracted even at consenting to my opinions. In reality, he was making contact with his inner self, his internal world with the music matter already in store. Nino was extraordinarily creative in the hours after sunset; he could detach himself from a conversation, go to the piano and, like a medium, begin to play. You could feel that he had lost contact, he no longer followed nor heard you, it seemed that further explanations and details were obstacles to his creative process. If I liked a particular motif, he punctually replied, "I do not remember it already." We had to use a tape recorder on many occasions in order to capture those improvisations without Nino's knowledge, otherwise the "celestial" contact was lost. Working with him was a real joy. His flow of creativity was such that he elated you to the extent that you began to believe you were actually composing the music yourself. He truly got inside my characters and situations, permeating them with his music. For me, Nino was one of the three, four musicians of our time. He was a total musician. I have read some negative reviews about him which I find ridiculous. He lived in music as in the most spontaneously congenial environment. Our understanding as a team was such that we risked the most Draconian deadlines with success. The assurance that everything was going to be fine never abandoned us. I remember a unique image of Rota in a huge recording studio, a full orchestra, technicians and cables and microphones everywhere. In the midst of the recording session I saw Nino leaping among the music stands, reaching the oboist and, pencil in hand, making an emendation in the oboe part. Those were the "miracles" of Nino Rota. I have not thought as yet about the fact that he is gone and that I am about to begin a new film without him. For now, I don't wish to think about it. I cannot separate his presence from mine, the way he approached the undertaking of scoring my films. He came at the end, when the stress provoked by shooting, dubbing, etc...had reached its peak. But, as soon as he arrived, the stress disappeared and everything was transformed into a feast; the film entered a happy, serene, fantastic zone, an atmosphere in which it received a new life. It was always a surprise when, at the end of the making of a film, after so much stress and months of work, Nino, looking at the screen, would say, "Who is that actor?" "He is the protagonist," I would say. And the thought of a film of mine without his music not only for *La città delle donne* but for subsequent films as well, but maybe it is a thought dictated by the deep feelings of the moment...Ours was a friendship of sounds. In recent times I preferred that the music for certain sequences was ready before shooting. Especially for *La città delle donne* which contains some Broadway-type musical scenes. But Nino was not well. He suffered from a heart ailment, and although I was scheduled to start on April 26, I hesitated to call on him, despite my thought that work could have been beneficial to him. For the past ten days he was saying that he was ready, but I continued to hesitate. Monday morning I phoned him by saying: "I cannot come this evening either, I promised Fabrizio Clerici to attend his exhibit at *Ca' d'Oro* in *Via Condotti*, and I cannot avoid going. We will do the music as soon as I start shooting." While I was at the exhibit, I saw him facing me. He was pale, more than usual, and with a vaguely reproaching tone he said to me: "You have become a vagabond. You are not thinking of letting someone also write the soundtrack of *La città delle donne* are you?" We scheduled a meeting for Tuesday at our usual meeting place, Rota's house in *Piazza delle Coppelle*. I was just about to leave Cinecittá to get to his place when a friend phoned me to tell me that Nino was no more.

What else could I say? I could say so many things after thirty years of collaboration. His main characteristic was a sort of levitation, a presence-absence kind of thing. I had this feeling when I paid my last respects to him at the *Clinica del Rosario*. For the first time I had the sensation that a man had disappeared. Not died, had disappeared – which I reflected was the impression I had had of Nino when he was alive."

[This testimonial entitled *L'amico magico* was published in *Il messaggero* on April 13, 1979. The English translation is mine]

THE FELLINI-ROTA PERIOD (1952-1979)

This comparative table lists films by Fellini and other director for which Nino Rota composed the music. Titles marked in bold letters refer to concert and stage works.

FELLINI	OTHER FILMS, CONCERT WORKS, OPERAS
1952	
Lo sceicco bianco	*Jolanda, la figlia del corsaro nero* (Mario Soldati)
	I tre corsari (Mario Soldati)
	Un ladro in paradiso (Domenico Paolella)
	Marito e moglie (Eduardo De Filippo)
	Noi due soli (Girolami, Marchi, Metz)
	Fanciulle di lusso (Bernard Vorhaus)
	La regina di Saba (Pietro Francisci)
1953	
I vitelloni	*Anni facili* (Luigi Zampa)
	Variazioni sopra un tema gioviale (1953)
	L'amante di Paride (Marc Allegret)
	La domenica della buona gente

(Anton Giulio Majano)
La mano dello straniero
(Mario Soldati)
La nave delle donne maledette
(Raffaello Matarazzo)
Il nemico pubblico No. 1
(Henry Verneuil)
Riscatto o tu sei il mio giudice
(Marino Girolami)
Scampolo '53
(Giorgio Bianchi)
I sette dell'Orsa Maggiore
(Duilio Coletti)
Boulanger de Valorgue
(Henry Verneuil)
Melodie immortali o Mascagni
(Giacomo Gentilomo)
Gli uomini che mascalzoni
(Glauco Pellegrini)

1954

La strada

Via Padova 46 o Lo scocciatore
(Giorgio Bianchi)
Appassionatamente
(Giacomo Gentilomo)
Bella, non piangere
(David Carbonari)
Cento anni d'amore
(Lionello De Felice)
Divisione Folgore
(Duilio Coletti)

Le due orfanelle
(Giacomo Gentilomo)
La grande speranza
(Duilio Coletti)
Mambo
(Robert Rossen)
Musoduro
(Giuseppe Bennati)
Proibito
(Mario Monicelli)
The Star of India
(Arthur Lubin and Edoardo Anton)
Senso
(Luchino Visconti)

1955

Il bidone

Accadde al penitenziario
(Giorgio Bianchi)
Il cappello di paglia di Firenze (1944-55)
Amici per la pelle
(Franco Rossi)
La bella di Roma
(Luigi Comencini)
Un eroe dei nostri tempi
(Mario Monicelli)
La via del successo...con le donne o, Io piaccio
(Giorgio Bianchi)

1956

Città di notte
(Leopoldo Trieste)
War and Peace

(King Vidor)
Londra chiama Polo Nord
(Duilio Coletti)

1957

Le notti di Cabiria

Italia piccola
(Mario Soldati)
Sinfonia No. 3 (1956-57)
Gli italiani sono matti
(Duilio Coletti)
Il medico e lo stregone
(Mario Monicelli)
Il momento piú bello
(Lucino Emmer)
La diga sul Pacifico
(René Clement)

1958

Un ettaro di cielo
(Aglauco Casadio)
La legge è legge
(Christian-Jacque)
Fortunella
(Eduardo De Filippo)

1959

Plein Soleil
(René Clement)
La grande guerra
(Mario Monicelli)

1960
La dolce vita

Femmine di lusso
(Giorgio Bianchi)
Concerto per orchestra (1959-61)
Fantasia sopra 12 note del Don Giovanni di Mozart (1960)
Rocco e i suoi fratelli
(Luchino Visconti)
Sotto dieci bandiere
(Duilio Coletti)

1962
Le tentazioni del Dottor Antonio
[Boccaccio '70]

Il lavoro [Boccaccio '70]
(Luchino Visconti)
Mysterium (1962)
The Reluctant Saint
(Edward Dmytryk)
The Best of Enemies
(Guy Hamilton)

1963
Otto e mezzo

Il Gattopardo
(Luchino Visconti)
Il maestro di Vigevano
(Eliko Petri)
Concerto per archi (1964)

1965
Giulietta degli spiriti

L'ora di punta
[Oggi, domain, dopodomani]
(Eduardo De Filippo)
Aladino e la lampada magica (1965)

1966

Spara forte, più forte...non capisco
(Eduardo De Filippo)
La strada. [Ballet] (1966)

1967
Toby Dammit
[Tre passi nel delirio]

Romeo e Giulietta
(Franco Zeffirelli)

1969
Satyricon

La vita di Maria (1969-70)

1970
I clowns

Waterloo
(Sergej Fedorovich Bondarchuk)

1971

The Godfather
(Francis Ford Coppola)
Roma Capomunni (1970-71)

1972
Roma

Concerto per violoncello No. 1 (1972)

1973
Amarcord

Film d'amore e d'anarchia
(Lina Wertmüller)
Napoli milionaria (1973-77)

		Sunset Sunrise
		(Akira Kurohara)
1974		*The Godfather* (Part II)
		(Francis Ford Coppola)
		The Abdication
		(Anthony Harvey)
1976		
	Il Casanova	*Caro Michele*
		(Mario Monicelli)
		Le Molière imaginaire. [Ballet] (1976)
		Il ragazzo di borgata
		(Giulio Paradisi)
1978		*Death on the Nile*
		(John Guillermin)
		La dodicesima notte. [Incidental Music] (1978-79)
1979		
	Prova d'orchestra	*The Hurricane*
		(Jan Troell)

PART TWO

THE FILM *AMARCORD* (1973)
INTRODUCTION

As stated earlier, when, in 1952, Federico Fellini first proposed that Rota write the soundtrack for *Lo sceicco bianco*, the musician had already provided music for over 60 Italian and foreign motion pictures; therefore, he was hardly "discovered" by the future-great filmmaker. The misperception can be detected in many writings on Fellini whenever Rota's music is mentioned, and in Fellini's own interviews and conversations. It is known that Fellini was a *raconteur par excellence*, so his references to Rota are often embellished in one way or another, notwithstanding the fact that he had the greatest admiration and a sincere love for Nino. However, would anyone today be curious about Rota's music if it were not for Fellini's films? John Simon has pointed, in a recent article, that the actual great number of recordings of Rota's concert music permits a fair discovery of the composer's versatility. The critic, in fact, encourages his readers to go and discover for themselves such a patrimonium in which "abundant moments of serenity are guaranteed."[1] There is, indeed, much great music in the 145 film scores and over 100 concert compositions which constitute Rota's output, but it was only for Fellini's films that Rota's music was special. His music so much penetrated the director's poetics that the impression was that the music was composed by Fellini himself, in the Griffith-Chaplin tradition.[2] The symbiosis between music and images here is such that one element becomes indivisible from the other.[3] This phenomenon is less evident in Rota's other collaborations, even with artists like Luchino Visconti, Lina Wertmüller, Eduardo De Filippo, Franco Zeffirelli and Francis Ford Coppola or, in instances when a celebrated Fellini

---

[1] Simon, John. "The Other Rota" in *The New Criterion*, September 2000: 53-59.
[2] Charles Chaplin's tunes were molded and put into practical form by various composers including David Raksin. See David Raksin, "Life with Charlie" in *Library of Congress Quarterly* XL/3 Summer 1983: 234-53. For Charles Griffith's musical ideas see Martin Miller Marks. *Music and Silent Film: Contexts & Case Studies 1895-1924* (New York: Oxford University Press, 1997).
[3] See Andrea Lee, "Really Fellini." *The New Yorker*. Dec. 11, 1995: 94-100.

script and the music written for it transmigrated to another medium, as in the case of the ballet *La strada*.[4]

Amarcord. What does this name mean? In the dialect spoken in the Emilia-Romagna region of Central Italy it means "I remember" in its reflexive form. It is better translated in Italian as A (Io) m (mi) 'arcord (ricordo). However, the "I" soon becomes "We" as collective memories turn into a proud socio-anthropological affirmation of national belonging.

This is a film in which Fellini remembered or, rather, reinvented his life as a teenager in his native town of Rimini around the year 1935. It is an entertaining and melancholy view of provincial life in a provincial Italy between the wars-- when Mussolini's Fascism, the Church and the Royal House of Savoia exercised power, especially on the "little" people. Results often were not too positive: Tribal families, inadequate schools, sexual repression, prison-like mental hospitals, and a political regime which resorted to "paternalistic," unorthodox methods to convince stubborn citizens that Fascism was, after all, a way of life to everybody's benefit.

Fellini does not seem displeased in recounting his past, which is the past of all the Italians of his generation. After all, he is remembering youth, thus celebrating a season of life which will never return again, a precious time in one's earthly sojourn. Keep in mind that Fellini portrays life in the Adriatic resort town of Rimini which, as provincial as it probably was in 1935 (not today by all means), was not a backward area somewhere in the *Mezzogiorno* or on the Islands. In *Amarcord* Fellini emphasizes the comic, the grotesque aspects of life which make the film understandable by viewers from different cultures. The gallery of portraits and anecdotes in the film can provoke different readings, as we shall see in the course of this chapter. Fellini, however, did not seem to want to pass any judgment on his past's narrative nor was he willing to propose a solution to the political situation in which his characters strove. For those who grew up in the post-war years in small towns, Fellini's stories helped reconstruct

---

[4] This ballet, commissioned by La Scala for famous ballerina Carla Fracci, was given its premiere on September 2, 1966. Besides themes from the celebrated Fellini's film, it incorporated material from other movies such as *Rocco e i suoi fratelli* and more.

memories. For others, more or less fortunate, Fellini is not only a wonderful storyteller but a first-class poet. *Amarcord* begins and ends with the celebration of the Winter equinox. As the four seasons unfold, the spectator is left with a sense of longing, a dream-like state which, for many, is a voyage into collective memories. Through it, Rota's music and its orchestration provide, with disarming simplicity, the ideal framework for the many "solo" and "choral" portraits in the film.

STRUCTURE, MEANING AND CRITICISM

Cast of Characters:

Titta [Bruno Zanin], Miranda (Titta's mother) [Pupella Maggio], Aurelio (Titta's father) [Armando Brancia], Oliva (Titta's brother) [Stefano Proietti] Lallo (Titta's uncle) [Nandino Orfei], Grandfather [Giuseppe Ianigro], Uncle Teo [Ciccio Ingrassia], Gina, the housekeeper [Carla Mora], Gradisca [Magali Noël], Volpina [Josiane Tanzilli], Tobacconist [Maria Antonietta Beluzzi], Biscein [Antonio Spaccatini], Giudizio [Gennaro Ombra], Naso [Alvaro Vitali], Ovo [Bruno Scagnetti], Gigliozzi [Bruno Lenzi], Candela [Francesco Vona] Bobo [Lino Patruno] Ciccio [Fernando De Felice], Aldina [Donatella Gambini], Zeus the headmaster [Francesco Magno], Philosophy teacher [Mauro Misul], Math teacher [Dina Adorni], Physics teacher [Francesco Maselli], Greek teacher [Ferdinando Villella], Art History teacher [Fides Stagni], Don Balosa [Gianfilippo Carcano], Ronald Colman owner of movie theatre [Ferruccio Brembilla], Cantarel the blind accordion player [Domenico Pertica], Lawyer [Luigi Rossi]. Count of Lovignano [Antonino Faá di Bruno], Count's daughter [Carmela Eusepi], Young Count Poltavo [Gianfranco Marrocco], Madonna, the coachman [Fausto Signoretti], Prince [Marcello di Falco].

****

Amarcord first appeared in print in 1973 as a novel by Federico Fellini and Tonino Guerra.[5] The film script, reconstructed by Liliana Betti by viewing it at the moviola in 1973, was published the following year prior to the film's distribution. This book, entitled *Il film Amarcord* was edited by Gianfranco Angelucci and Liliana Betti.[6] It is a collection of essays on the subject to serve as an introduction to the reconstructed script of the film. Apparently, there is no original (manu)script available. The book opened with Angelucci's dense résumé of Fellini's films to 1974, which he appropriately entitled "Fellini 15 1/2 e la poetica dell'onirico." It is followed by "Il mio paese" by Federico Fellini, perhaps the director's original book of memoirs of his native town. This short story appeared in English with the title "Rimini, my home town" in *Fellini on Fellini* (New York, N.Y.: Delacorte Press, 1976); it was then published in 1987 as *La mia Rimini*, edited by Renzo Bianchi for the publisher Cappelli of Bologna. What follows is a brief colloquium between Fellini and Enzo Siciliano entitled "In teatro persino il mare" which had previously appeared in *Il Mondo* of September 13, 1973 under the title "Fellini: io e il film." Finally, there is an interview by Valerio Riva entitled "Il fascismo dentro di noi."

Riva's article had also previously appeared in *L'Espresso* of October 7, 1973 under the title "La balia in camicia nera," thus making it the earliest published discussion of *Amarcord*. This article has been published in English, translated by Peter Bondanella with the title "The Fascism within Us: An Interview with Valerio Riva" in "Federico Fellini: Essays in Criticism."[7]

Since this sort of "Urtext" description of the film was published before distribution, it should be taken into consideration first. Both the original title of this interview, "La balia in camicia nera" ("The Nanny in Black Shirt"), and "Il fascismo dentro di noi" ("The Fascism within Us"), attest to the political connotation of the film. In Fellini's words: "Fascism is not viewed, as in most political films that are made today, from (how can I put it) a judgmental

---

[5] See Fellini and Tonino Guerra. *Amarcord* (Milano: Rizzoli, 1973) 3rd. 1974.
[6] Angelucci, Gianfranco and Liliana Betti. *Il film Amarcord di Federico Fellini* (Bologna: Cappelli, 1974).
[7] Riva, Valerio. "The Fascism within Us: An Interview with Valerio Riva." In *Federico Fellini: Essays in Criticism* (P. Bondanella, ed.) (New York: Oxford University Press, 1978): 20-26.

perspective. That is, from the outside. Detached judgments, antiseptic diagnoses, complete and definitive formulae always seem to me (at least on the part of those of the generation to which I belong) a bit inhuman." The entire film, Fellini continues, rotates in Jungian terms around the episode in which the *Federale* (the Province's secretary of the fascist party) arrives in town on an official visit. He, therefore, represents *Il Duce* to the "little" people. The entire population then shows its eternal state of adolescence. "I have the impression," Fellini says, "that Fascism and adolescence continue to be, in a certain measure, permanent historical seasons of our lives: adolescence of our individual lives, Fascism of our national lives. That is, this remaining children for eternity, this leaving responsibilities for others with a sensation that there is someone who thinks for you (mother, father, the mayor, *Il Duce*, another time the Bishop or the Madonna) in short, other people. I believe, that even before Fascism, the fault of this chronic insufficient development, this arrested development at a childlike stage, lies with the Catholic Church."

Concerning the name *Amarcord*, Fellini is very careful to explain that it does not mean "I remember at all; instead, it is a kind of cabalistic word, a word of seduction, the brand of an aperitif..." He does not wish the film to be taken as autobiographical. In fact, he goes on to say that he wants to entitle it simply *Viva l'Italia* or *Il borgo* in the sense of a medieval enclosure, a lack of information, a lack of contact with the unheard of, the new. *Amarcord*, in its mystery, means only the feeling that characterizes the whole film: a funereal feeling, one of isolation, dream, torpor, and of ignorance.

Aldo Tassone's essay published in *La Revue du Cinema: Image et Son* No. 290 (1974), pp.17-38 and then published in Julia Conaway Bondanella's English translation in *Fellini: Essays in Criticism* under the title "From Romagna to Roma: The Voyage of a Visionary Chronicler (Roma and Amarcord)," writes that in the 1970's, Fellini leaned nostalgically upon his past, his biography acting as a filter, a spyglass which he used to better capture life as it was.[8] Concerning *Amarcord*, Tassone quotes Fellini: "I want to create a tableau-portrait without precise temporal connotations. Perhaps because I no longer succeed in distinguishing past, present and future." But Tassone writes, "Fellini makes us discover familiar things as if we were looking at them for the first time with the eyes of infancy." Well put. Fellini, in fact, sets up a series of "things seen" gathered together by a metaphysical eye and organizes them into a voyage toward another reality.

Tassone links *Amarcord* to *I clowns* and *Roma* to form a trilogy, not simply because "the three films belong to a sort of quest, but also that the same conspiratorial irony, the same melancholy, the same tendency to fantastic expansion of chronicle unite them." In *Amarcord* the critic sees three main sequences:

1. Episode of the *Rex*, symbolizing collective myth.
2. Episode of the Autumn fog, symbolizing mystery.
3. Episode of Uncle Teo, symbolizing fabulous evasion.

The passing of the *Rex* is a scene of general excitement. Nothing ever happens in the provinces and one always lives in the expectation of something. Different from other "choral" scenes in the film, here the community waits for the unknown, the portent, the apparition of Mussolini's ocean liner, the power of Fascism. Consider Tassone's picturesque description of the episode: "This marvelous collective dream parades beneath the delighted eyes of the "Amarcordians" who make it the multifaceted symbol of everything they lack and all that they would like to have. This aquatic comet then moves away and leaves the "Amarcordians" in the most total obscurity." The scene of collective stupor is immediately followed by the scene of the Great Fog which erases everything, embodying the void. "The evocation of the magic of the seasons - one of the

---

[8] Tassone, Aldo. "From Romagna to Roma: The Voyage of a Visionary Chronicler (*Roma* and *Amarcord*)." In *Federico Fellini: Essays in Criticism* (P. Bondanella, ed.) (New York: Oxford University Press, 1978): 261-288.

novelties of the film - is of an extraordinary poetic vitality." Tassone continues, "*Amarcord* could be entitled *The Seasons of Our Illusions*. Fellini has done for cinema what Brueghel and Vivaldi did for painting and music. For Teo, a fool "ma non troppo," the countryside represents liberty. He is a prototype of a category of misfits or original characters. In this great circus of life, these extraordinary beings have the task - in Fellini's perspective - of bringing messages from another world. They do what the others no longer know how to do. This sequence, the most original in *Amarcord*, is the fusion of realism with magic, picaresque and mythical levels."

Allan H. Pasco's study "The Thematic Structure of Fellini's *Amarcord*,"[9] begins with the suggestion that the film is concerned with the survival of a human rather than a bestial man, viewed in a past which is very present, "a past that reminds us of our inability to learn from history and yet one which stresses man's most promising qualities." Pasco's conception is filtered through the film's two major themes: reality and illusion, each of which unfolds for the spectator as conflicts between true human values and dreams, whether sexual, intellectual, religious or political. Unlike other critics, Pasco makes much of the film characters' names and their significance. *Volpina*, for instance, the local nymphomaniac, has an "eerie resemblance to the fox her name suggests." For *Gradisca*, "receive with pleasure," the author recounts the episode with the prince whom he identifies as a caricature of Prince Umberto of the House of Savoia. Pasco does not miss an opportunity to unleash nasty comments on the Savoia's lackluster performance during Mussolini's regime and the spineless figures cut by both King Vittorio Emanuele III and his son, Umberto, after *Il Duce* was put out of office in 1943. The Savoias, Pasco concludes, "dashed the hopes of so many anti-fascist Italians and were partially accountable for the 1943-1945 bloody civil war." *Aurelio*, whose name means "golden," renders himself constantly ridiculous in his attempts to keep his son down and thus maintain the rather tarnished paternal "aura." *Titta* (a shortened form of Battista) has a number of significant

---

[9] Pasco, H. Allan. "The Thematic Structure of Fellini's *Amarcord*." *Film Studies Annual* (Ben Lawton, ed.) (West Lafayette, IN: Purdue University, 1976): 259-71.

experiences; he does indeed, "receive a baptism of sorts." *Miranda* bears the appropriate meaning of "admirable." For *Giudizio*, "Judgment," Pasco makes reference to Fellini's use of symbolism by bringing up the meanings of certain common keys in the Tarot. *Teo*, whose name is a common variant of the Greek etymon for God, is viewed as a character in limbo, more in touch with the "above" than with his peers. Regarding *Lucia*, the tobacconist, Pasco writes the following, "Though four oxen were reportedly unable to drag the sturdy Saint Lucia of the early Church to a brothel, *Titta* manages to lift the substantial tobacconist of the same name and to do it repeatedly." *Lallo*, nicknamed Pataca, a worthless piece of junk, because of his considering almost everything of real value as a "pataca" is the highest "pataca" himself and a "worthy" representative of those unforgettable characters Fellini created in "I vitelloni"(large calves feeding off the maternal cow long after the time has come to forage for themselves).

Curiously enough, some of the above mentioned names were different in Fellini and Tonino Guerra's original story.[10] *Titta*, for instance was *Bobo*; *Aurelio* was *Amedeo*; *Lucia* was nameless and *Teo* was *Leo*. Pasco concludes his engaging analysis by adding another significant aspect of *Amarcord*, the theme of rebirth, when he writes, "Fellini's *Amarcord* has an insistent message which is currently out of style: it encourages procreation, and it places an aura around the heads of mothers. Simultaneously, it warns of the emasculating dreams that could destroy us."

Louis D. Giannetti's essay, "*Amarcord*: The Impure Art of Federico Fellini,"[11] begins with a review of the negative criticism Fellini had been subjected to since *8 1/2*, especially from those critics who had dismissed his latest movies as formless and undisciplined. Fellini, Giannetti writes " has become the *monstre sacrée* of the contemporary cinema, the undisciplined "genius" for whom generous allowance must be made." The writer reminds those critics that, like Godard, Fellini de-emphasized objective linear narrative in favor

---

[10] See Note # 5.
[11] Giannetti, Louis D. "*Amarcord*: The Impure Art of Federico Fellini." *Western Humanities Review* 30 (1976): 153-58.

of thematic leitmotifs which, in his case, are in part mosaically structured. In his discussion of the film Giannetti provides a rather *sui generis* interpretation of the name *Amarcord* , it represents, he writes, " a linguistic fusion of AMO (I love) and AMARO (bitter) with MI RICORDO (I remember)." Now, if everyone assumes as Giannetti does, that the "I" is Fellini himself, then the movie becomes a sort of bittersweet, stylized documentary. Having stated this; Giannetti shows perplexity about the issue of narration throughout the film. Tassone's interpretation, on the other hand, is that *Amarcord* does not mean "I remember" but that in Fellini's mind signified "Do you remember?" or simply "once upon a time" as in the beginning of any fable; therefore, Fellini does not document in the Griersonian sense but rather "celebrates" facts, people, and places. Giannetti observes that *Amarcord* is not a year in the lives of the citizens of Rimini during the Fascist period, but Fellini's "poetically stylized remembrance of things past, in a film unified by a dense substructure of leitmotifs related to the seasons as well as the age of the protagonists, youth to maturity to death to rebirth."

Like Tassone, Giannetti finds the episode of the *Rex* to be the most moving sequence in the film. It opens in daytime, which Fellini characteristically associates with comedy and earthly vulgarity, and ends late at night, which is generally associated with solitude, spirituality, and aspiration. Giannetti points out the juxtaposition of what is called in this book "choral" or community ritualistic scenes such as the bonfire, the *Rex*, the funeral service and procession, Gradisca's wedding and the "solo" or individual scenes in the film when private dreams are, Giannetti says, "generally associated with romantic fantasies, usually in some sexual form, but like most of the characters' aspirations, these fantasies are essentially masturbatory." Returning to the question of autobiography, Giannetti concludes "that Fellini managed to portray himself through his characters, and, in retrospect, he is able to see his characters in himself. And it's no small measure of his genius that he also succeeds in permitting us to see ourselves in him/them, and him/them in ourselves."

Millicent Marcus' heartfelt essay "*Amarcord* : Film As Memory,"[12] deals with the film's various kinds of memory: autobiographical, historical, literary, and cinematographic. She sees Fellini as the teenaged Titta, guiding the viewer through the movie, introducing the town, its collective character and even the self-appointed "cicerone" who might look suspiciously like Fellini himself. Historical memories are evoked by the recurring rhetorical patterns of Fascism which Marcus describes as "a twisted memory of the Roman Empire, filtered through the mind of a latter-day Caesar. By appropriating only the external trappings of antiquity, without an understanding of the cultural forces which made Rome possible, Mussolini betrayed his flawed memory of the imperial past." The pivotal social function of the Cinema Fulgor is much highlighted in this essay, showing how the power of the cinema can generate its own myths and memories, in this case the power of seduction American cinema exercised on the townspeople. So, Marcus writes, "*Amarcord* constitutes a crucial link in the ongoing chain of cinema-memory-cinema." The concept of memory is also emphasized by the author in her interpretation of the name Amarcord. " Fellini's use of dialect in the title reveals the personal, idiosyncratic quality of this story, while his choice of a reflexive verb ("Io mi ricordo" in standard Italian) rather than a transitive one suggests the mind's action upon itself as it turns inward in memory."

Literary memories are evoked by the seasonal periodicity of the episodes and Fellini's presentation of a panorama of literary genres. Marcus observes that "the opening sequence in the spring is satiric, with splendid vignettes of schoolroom pranks. The summer is romantic, as we follow the fragmented tale of how *La Gradisca* got her name, and how the candy man seduced a harem. Autumn is ironic, as the family takes the lunatic Uncle Teo on a disastrous outing in the country. Winter is tragic with the death of Miranda, and spring brings a comic ending with the marriage of *La Gradisca* to her chubby *carabiniere*." I would like to note here that the actor playing the carabiniere is the same who played the valet in *La Gradisca*'s meeting with the prince episode. Since the

---

[12] Marcus, Millicent. "Fellini's *Amarcord*: Film as Memory." *Quarterly Review of Film Studies* 2 (1977): 418-25.

authenticity of the encounter was in doubt among the townspeople, the story could have happened only in *La Gradisca*'s fantasy. Therefore, marrying a *carabiniere*, after all a man in uniform, a member of the Royal Guard, constitutes her only romantic reality. Like all other critics commenting on *Amarcord*, Marcus is taken by the *Rex* episode; this time, though, she singles out an important character, the blind accordionist. She writes, "Fellini embodies his musical theme in the blind accordion player who performs Nino Rota's songs throughout the movie. This figure, himself unseeing, constitutes an important visual image for us - sitting on his stool, playing away on his accordion, throwing his head back in utter abandon to his music. Our hearts nearly break when he, too, goes to see the *Rex* and cries out "what does she look like," taking his dark glasses off "to see better" we might add. Millicent Marcus concludes her brilliant essay on film and memory by stating that "filmmaking becomes a technological analogue for the very dynamic of memory. So *Amarcord* is not only a film of reminiscence, it is a film as reminiscence. The medium is the memory." Emotional unity-synthesis of what is remembered and what is seen.

Parshall's essay "Fellini's Thematic Structuring: Patterns of Fascism in *Amarcord* "[13] is an appropriate segue to Giannetti's article. In fact, the author begins his discussion by quoting Giannetti's observation that *Amarcord* like *Satyricon* and *Roma* are not just "tossed together" as some critics suggested; because, he writes, "along with Godard, Fellini is one of the supreme formalists of the contemporary cinema. Like Godard he has de-emphasized objective linear narrative in favor of thematic leitmotifs which are structured mosaically." Consequently, Parshall examines that mosaic structure. Against a backdrop discussing the circumstances that caused "Italy's pre-war drift into fascism," then, by taking the *Federale*'s visit to the town which Fellini himself had indicated as a "central, irreplaceable, indispensable episode," Parshall installs the theme of Fascism as a central nexus in order to discover, he says, "how tightly unified the apparently disjointed scenes are." Parshall, faithful to his chosen course of

---

[13] Parshall, Peter F. "Fellini's Thematic Structures: Patterns of Fascism in Amarcord." *Film Criticism* 7, #2 (1983): 19-30.

investigation, begins his analysis with the episode of the fascist rally which follows the church confession and sexual fantasies of the boys. The author, therefore, identifies a link between immature sexuality and Fascism. This thesis starts to unfold during the rally when *Lallo* discusses with his running mates the size of Mussolini's testicles, a supreme asset of masculinity, a notion often recurring in Italian culture. Gabriele D'Annunzio, for instance, was always proud to announce to one of his female interlocutors, Ada Mainardi Colleoni, wife of cellist Enrico Mainardi and Toscanini's lover, that he was indeed endowed with the "triplice coglia" like her famous ancestor, condottiero Bartolomeo Colleoni [coglioni], hence his name.[14] The unfolding continues with *Gradisca*, representing the town's feminine sexuality, particularly when she runs along the edge of the crowd begging "Oh, let me touch him," referring to the *Federale*, i.e. *Il Duce*. This leads to another consideration: sexuality and man in military uniform. *Gradisca* fell in love with Gary Cooper's foreign legionnaire's uniform in *Beau Geste*; she is then dazzled by the very elegant uniform of the prince in the alleged adventure at the Grand Hotel and, finally, marries a man in uniform, an ordinary *carabiniere*. *Volpina* portrays psychotic sexuality as the town's nymphomaniac who enjoys masturbatory pleasures by urinating on the beach while being watched by nearby workers. And then there is the tobacconist with her enormous breasts, symbolizing a superwoman, just as Mussolini's testicles symbolize the notion of a superman, a frequent equation in Fellini's movies. Even the car race, *Le mille miglia*, crossing town in the middle of the night, could be interpreted as a form of collective "penetration" like the passing of the roaring motorcyclist, another recurring leitmotif which Parshall describes as possessing the type of "aggressive sexuality that, once changed into aggressive behavior, can become fascistic." Sexual connotations are also detected in various feeding scenes: *Miranda* feeding the family juxtaposed to the fascists force feeding castor oil to *Aurelio*; the tobacconist forcing *Titta* to suck her nipples, juxtaposed with *Miranda* nursing the feverish *Titta* after his traumatic sexual encounter with *Lucia* in the tobacco shop. Likewise, the fulfilling dinner in the country which provokes

---

[14] Pizzetti, Bruno. *Ildebrando Pizzetti: Cronologia e Bibliografia* (Parma: La Pilotta, 1980): 225.

Uncle Teo's memorable utterances from the top of a tree as he shouts at the top of his lungs, "Voglio una donna!" A logical conclusion which reminds this writer of a similar episode in Rita Wertmüller's *Film d'amore e d'anarchia* (1973), also with music by Rota, when the *Comandante* tells his guests dining in the country that after having "drunk, eaten, farted, pissed, shat and fucked" it was time for everybody to return to the city. Parshall also sees a juxtaposition between the Catholic Church and the Fascist Party, following Fellini's assertion that they are both authoritarian systems. The Church being "a somewhat gentler form of fascism and fascism being a kind of religion."[15] This notion is pointed out in the essay several times in reference to the portraits of the Pope and Mussolini hanging on the walls of public institutions. It is interesting to note that there was always the picture of the King to complete the trio, an often neglected, yet important, dimension in Italy's political and civic life. Naturally, this attitude was also linked to the other major social institutions - the school and the family.

In schools we see Fascist doctrine taught in line with religion, and, in the family, even an anarchist like *Aurelio* becomes a little *Duce* when the occasion arises to impose his views upon other members of the household. Then, observe *Don Balosa*, the priest, doing the same thing in his church. Therefore, Fellini shows, Parshall writes, "that all the major social institutions - church, school, family - support Fascism because they are themselves authoritarian systems and consequently produce the immature persons which Fascism attracts...all the pranks in the film - including particularly the incidents involving urination, defecation, and flatulence - show rebellion against authority in an ineffective and immature way, permitting the system to continue its domination. *Amarcord* hus concisely portrays the societal structures which made inevitable Fascism's domination in Italy." Toward the conclusion of his well developed and richly detailed essay, Parshall examines another connection - Fascism and death as emphasized in the film's two final ceremonies - *Miranda*'s funeral procession and *Gradisca*'s wedding . He writes, "Miranda's death seems to signal the loss of

---

[15] Gentile, Emilio. *Il culto del littorio* (Bari: Laterza, 1993). English version by Keith Botsford entitled *The Sacralization of Politics in Fascist Italy* (Cambridge, MA: Harvard University Press, 1996).

maternal caring and of Christian faith. By juxtaposition, the funeral also casts a pall on Gradisca's wedding, which has a melancholy tone." One is reminded that when *Lallo*, *Miranda*'s brother, passed out in church at his sister's funeral, *Aurelio*'s comment "Take him to the whorehouse!" means that with the passing of *Miranda*, sister-mother figure, only a whore-sister-mother figure could take care of him, not the rest of society, including his pals, "vitelloni." The wedding scene is conclusive in many ways: the recurrence of Spring, i.e., new life, the realization of *Gradisca*'s dream, such as it is, and the apparition of *Biscein* saying to the viewers: "Go home now; it is all finished." While the blind accordionist's music fades into infinity, everybody bids farewell to the newlyweds who take off in a boxy, black automobile.

James Hay is the author of a well-received book about Italian cinema during Fascism.[16] The book, taking Fellini's *Amarcord* as a point of departure, is of interest. A series of abstracts entitled "Grandfather Fascism and *Amarcord*" has been republished recently. Hay's treatment of the subject opens with a quotation taken from an interview Fellini granted to Corrado Augias for *Panorama* (January 14, 1980) entitled, "Ho inventato tutto. Anche me: conversazione con Federico Fellini," which in English reads, "I Have Invented Everything, Even Myself: A Conversation with Federico Fellini." Here Fellini states that "*Amarcord* is a study of the closed ethos of a boy who knew nothing of the world outside of his small Italian coast side village during the 1930's, for whom Fascism was just another imposition like his father, mother, priest or schoolteachers." Hay is of the opinion that "Fellini was unable to examine critically a part of history that was part of him, that constituted him." In structuralist terms, the author continues, "*Amarcord* demonstrates the manner in which social, political, and economic realities are explored, questioned, and shaped through a cultural mythology in the midst of crisis...Fellini "remembers" his childhood as a text , i.e., as a series of epiphanies or symbolically charged moments that are related and meaningful because they

---

[16] Hay, James. *Popular Film Culture in Fascist Italy: The Passing of the Rex* (Bloomington, IN: Indiana University Press, 1987).

are inextricable from a constellation of ever-present "second-order sign systems" or myths."

For Hay, the "Cinema Fulgor," the town movie theatre, is most important, beginning with the figure of its proprietor who looks and acts like Ronald Coleman. The movie house was then part of the community representing a window, perhaps the only window, to an outside world -- even if populated by images. The function of cinema (a relatively new and "marginal" form at that time in the Italian provinces) was to create "subtle yet profound strains in the town's fabric of consensus [to Fascism], making its traditional communal frameworks of interpretation appear contrived and absurd even to those who employ them. Thus, while cinema appears deeply embedded in the culture of this town, it also contributes to its rather "leaky" consensus."

Hay also places a great deal of emphasis on the ever-present photographer who is ready to document every ritual and spectacle in the town - the school picture, the Fascist rally, the celebration of St. Joseph's Day, the arrival of the caliph and his harem, the passing of the *Rex*, and *Gradisca*'s wedding banquet. In fact, the author writes, "*Amarcord* is very much about viewing (and reviewing) images, about image and spectator." In summarizing the functions of both cinema as image-spectacle and photography as image-document, Hay cites Roland Barthes, who claims a significant difference between cinema and photographic image, between something that "has posed" before the lens and something that "has passed" before it. *Amarcord*, the author concludes, "repeatedly combines and juxtaposes these effects." An interesting section of Hay's study deals with *Amarcord* as a political film *vis-à-vis* other Italian films of the 1970's set in the Fascist period. Following a substantial examination of several films by De Sica, Bartolucci, Pasolini, Scola, Wertmüller and others, the author reaches the conclusion that "contemporary films which examine the psychological undercurrents that may have sustained Fascism also lend support to the notion that it was not a historically specific phenomenon, that Italian filmmakers' preoccupation with Fascism was part of a more extensive dialogue among film critics and historians about the social and political function of cultural forms and about the traditional "prerogative" of Neorealism and of aesthetic criticism in general."

Hay views the episode of the Grand Hotel as a revolving door to the "*Bel Mondo*" perhaps as *Via Veneto* was for. *La dolce vita* Consequently, he compares films dealing with the codes and icons of the international cinema of the 1930's. As for *Amarcord*'s Grand Hotel, and especially for the teenager, *Titta*, who only sees the inside of it through a keyhole, he writes, "For the young Titta in Amarcord, the Grand Hotel is emblematic of cosmopolitan leisure, and the romance which that lifestyle affords." Considering that the passages described here are part of a volume, it would be appropriate to close by reiterating James Hay's purpose in reflecting on *Amarcord* in the context of a narrative dealing with Italian cinema of the 1920's and 1930's. He writes, "As a national-popular history, *Amarcord* is no less insightful or comprehensive a modeling of Fascist Italy than the reams of political and social histories on the subject. Its authority, however, may not be as readily accepted, since it continually questions its own authority, as historical narration, and deconstructs the historical reality of the regime. And, in this sense, it is a testament to the "postmodern" conditions that have compelled a rethinking and recontextualization of Fascism. It is largely for this reason that Amarcord serves as my point of departure."

The year 1990 marked the thirtieth anniversary of the release of *La dolce vita*. It was celebrated by a wave of essays, articles and interviews, defining this masterpiece, said Bondanella in *The Cinema of Federico Fellini*, "as a brilliant fresco of a new, media-conscious society that had emerged from the sleepy provincial culture of Italy in the 1950's and that had anticipated by at least a decade contemporary concerns over the domination of popular culture by mass media images, a theme continued and broadened in a number of Fellini's more recent metacinematic works to include what he considers to be the insidious influence of commercial television."

Federico Fellini died on October 31, 1993. Five months later, his wife of fifty years, actress Giulietta Masina, also died. It was the end of an era in Italian cinema and cinema in general; it is a pity that these two great masters did not live to be part of cinema's first centennial in 1996. The art of Fellini, the subject of abundant literature and inspiration to so many young filmmakers has been summarized and finally codified in a comprehensive and perhaps definitive study by Peter Bondanella, *The Cinema of Federico Fellini*.[17] In Fellini's own words, in the book's Foreword, "Bondanella's conclusions and proposals will serve to nourish independently of what I could write, an analytical discourse and a speculative dialectic that will, if nothing else, help to place the cinema in its true light among the arts." Indeed, Bondanella's book will inspire a new generation of studies about Fellini and on a host of peripheral topics.

Bondanella begins his discussion with two quotations which, although contradictory, do reach the same conclusion. The first is from Fellini himself: "I am not a political person, have never been one. Politics and sports leave me completely cold, indifferent." The second is from Lina Wertmüller: "Federico has given us the most significant traces and graffiti of our history in the last twenty years. He declares he is not concerned with politics and is not interested in fixed themes or ideological layouts, but he is, in the final analysis, the most political and sociological, I believe, of our authors." Then, the writer continues, "In *Amarcord* (Fellini's last major commercial success and the winner of an Oscar for Best Foreign Film, among dozens of other awards), Fellini combines a nostalgic look back at his own provincial origins with a relentless dissection of the origins of Italian fascism in a film that some critics initially defined as only a bittersweet remake of the provincial milieu of *I vitelloni*. As a portrait of the provincial world of the 1930's during Mussolini's reign, Fellini's *Amarcord* distinguishes itself from most other Italian films on the *ventennio* by its refusal to portray Italy's Fascist past through the prism of the "politically correct" Marxist or psychoanalytical ideologies so popular in the political film in Italy." Bondanella reiterates a concept as though he wishes to carve it in the reader's mind: "The unique emotional impact of *Amarcord* on audiences all over the world - and not just those Italian spectators whose age or nationality made them

---

[17] Bondanella, Peter. *The Cinema of Federico Fellini* (Princeton, NJ: Princeton University Press, 1992).

especially interested in the Fascist era - is a direct result of Fellini's refusal to produce a "political" film that intends merely to denounce an episode in Italy's history. Fellini's *Amarcord* departs from the typical portrayal of fascism in the Italian cinema, for both Fellini's memoirs and *Amarcord* avoid dividing the inhabitants of this Rimini of his imagination into "good" heroes (the anti-Fascists) and "bad" villains (the Fascists). Instead, the townspeople are sketched out in masterful caricature portraits as comic types all of whom have antecedents in Fellini's earlier works."

From this point, Bondanella engages in an analytical description of the characters and situations in the film. He finds the sequence devoted to *Gradisca* the most interesting, the one in which Fellini displays his metacinematic intentions as in the Cinema Fulgor episode: He writes, "As *Titta* moves from one seat to another, closer and closer to *Gradisca* with each successive cut, *Gradisca*, as if in a trance, stares at the silver screen, which displays a close-up of Gary Cooper from *Beau Geste,* a film made in 1939 but released in Italy only after the end of the war. Such a conscious anachronism plays up to the metacinematic intentions of the entire sequence...as we gaze at *Titta* as he gazes at *Gradisca* gazing at Gary Cooper we are provided with a double vision, enabling us to experience *Titta*'s "mystified perspective, while we judge it as the product of an inexperienced youth," wrote Millicent Marcus.[18] Bondanella concludes that, "We are prompted to evaluate both Titta and Gradisca as characters who relate to members of the opposite sex only through a form of mediated sexuality that originates in the cinema." The concept of metacinema is also evidenced in the episode of the *Rex* as Bondanella guides the reader through this much celebrated scene, from the moment when the people gather at the seashore to embark on small boats in order to sail out to meet the *Rex*, a sequence which is shot on location, to when "night draws nearer, we suddenly become aware that Fellini has shifted the scene from the ocean to a movie studio." The *Rex*, an ocean liner which indeed existed and was the pride of the regime, in Fellini's interpretation becomes, Bondanella says, "an artificial ocean liner painted on a billboard

---

[18] *Op. cit.*: 423.

construction near the *Cinecittá* pool with backlighting suggesting its port holes. As Fellini simulates the ship's passage by camera movements past the stationary set construction, his *Rex* seems to flop over into the water, revealing its status as both a product of cinematic artifice and as a false and mystifying image proposed by a regime founded on equally artificial ideas."

Concerning the film's political impact, Bondanella provides a fine analysis. Indeed, Bondanella's conclusive statement on this most remarkable film provides a fitting closure to this discussion of various published commentaries; "The extraordinary international success of *Amarcord* proved that Fellini's fictional interpretation of Italy's Fascist heritage had transcended mere historical re-creation...*Amarcord* stands as Fellini's most complex visual representation of a political theme, even though the ideological dimensions of the film do not exhaust its artistic achievements. Presenting a human comedy and transcending historical, ideological, or geographical boundaries, *Amarcord* speaks to our common humanity."

Frank Burke's volume *Fellini's Films, From Postwar to Postmodernism*,[19] posits the author's thesis clearly : "Fellini's most relevant work may prove to be not the modernist classics for which he is best known in North America, but his most recent postmodern work which has received limited distribution and recognition." With such a constant in mind, Burke assesses Fellini's early films in terms of postwar Western individualism and through evolving cold war rhetoric of individual freedom versus totalitarianism; in addition, he considers the death of individualism and the relation of Fellini's work to (high) modernism and postmodernism. Fellini, the author tells us, "fashioned his own brand of individualism as an anti-authoritarian response to his Fascist and Catholic upbringing." The road to salvation was not, Burke continues, "the Way of the Cross but the evolution of consciousness from the unconscious and the interpretation of all the fragmented and repressed aspects of the individual psyche." For this reason, he suggests that a close analysis of Fellini's individual films is the best

---

[19] Burke, Frank. *Fellini's Films: From Postwar to Postmodernism* (New York: Twayne Publishers, 1996).

way to explore the complex relations between representation and signification and modernism and postmodernism, rather than by any pre-established classification.

In his reading of *Amarcord*, Burke always places the reader-spectator within the realm of representation, even when he shifts the narrative outside the realm of art. Thus, by viewing various characters in the film, as "artists" and therefore "narrators" of their own life, *Amarcord* becomes a series of reconstructed memories. Burke begins his reading of the film by focusing on events and institutions central to the community: seasonal ritual, school, work, and family. Here he notices a great deal of rebelliousness within a great deal of conformity, recalling many memorable comic situations, such as school pranks and family squabbles. Collective attention is gathered at the arrival of external factors, like the new contingent of prostitutes and the "puffs," the swirling, floating seeds of springtime, which occupy everyone's attention and even control the narrative. Such a childish, innocent marvel beyond which Fellini so poetically portrays the torpor and boredom of provincial life, seems to irritate Burke. He, in fact, reads the phenomenon as a manifestation of the "absence of creative intelligence." Thus of *Giudizio*, he writes, "[he] is inarticulate in the extreme, having difficulty even repeating a simple rhyme associated with the puffs," and about the town lawyer, "[he] is a virtual parody of intelligence with his pedantic recitation of boring facts that merits an understandable anti-intellectualism from unseen hecklers." The critique of intelligence continues with the school episodes, in which Burke finds the students suffering "through a disjointed curriculum in which they nod their heads in unison to the tick tock' of a pendulum, mindlessly repeating the phrase ' pro-spet-tiva' (perspective), and recite meaningless facts and phrases on demand. Unable to exercise creative intelligence and self-expression in school, people turn to fantasy." In a footnote (#16, p. 360), Burke elaborates on the notion of perspective, " Although in *Juliet of the Spirits* the development of perspective is part of a gradual expansion of consciousness, here it suggests only the oppressive limiting of attention to a single, imposed point." An interesting observation, albeit misattributed in the reading; It is the "distracted" Art teacher who lectures about Giotto as the inventor of perspective and the Science teacher who illustrates the swinging of the pendulum.

Burke focuses more than once on what he refers to as the "mysterious motorcyclist" and his incursions in the community. The cyclist, he writes, " with no concrete ties to the town, seems to represent a kind of radical disconnectedness, in contrast to the community of night riders we saw at the end of *Roma*. The seeming alienation of the biker recalls another cyclist-powered Fellini's figure: *Zampanó*." The cyclist, whose face is always hidden by large glasses and helmet, although mysterious to us, the viewers, is not so to the "Amarcordians." He is, in fact, just another dysfunctional character responding to the nickname of *Scureza di Corpoló* (The fart of Corpoló) as *Giudizio* promptly regales him with an obscene rhyme which, this time, he has no problem to repeating: *Scureza, Scureza di Corpoló, in culo lo piglia e io glielo dó!* (The fart of Corpoló, when he gets it in his ass, I am the one giving it to him). Toward the end of the film, *Titta, Gradisca* and *Scureza* perform a delightful trio by chasing each other among the snowbanked corridors which had turned the town into a labyrinth. Fellini's sui generis mythological recreation of Theseus, Ariadne and the Mino-[Cen]taur? Perhaps!

A strong aspect of Burke's reading is his assessment of the representation of female sexuality, beginning with the boys contemplating the naked behind of a female statue part of a monument to World War One, symbolizing Victory (Vittoria), The boys, Burke points out, "are positioned behind 'her,' indicating a withdrawal from any direct encounter with women or even their representations." This is the first sustained instance in the film, the author continues, " of women reduced to fetishized body parts, and it is also part of the growing derriere mentality in Fellini's work, constructing women as inaccessible." So a major scoring point for *Lallo* occurs as he proudly announces, as noticed earlier in this book, that he has won a female tourist's anal intimacy. Burke equates the emergence of Fascism as replacing "the idealization of women in a manner that suggests the strong interplay of sexuality, repression, idealization, dependency, and power," and, turning to the most memorable utterance in the film, *Teo*'s

"*Voglio una donna*," Burke clarifies that *una donna*, in effect signifies only simulation, not woman or even desire for a woman. He writes, "Once woman as signifier is detached from woman as physical presence or possibility, *una donna* can even become equated with male power. Accordingly, *Teo* concludes his presence in the film completely submissive to a domineering, foul-mouthed, midget nun (Teo does get his donna, after all) summoned from the asylum and representative of male religious and medical institutions."

Burke views the *Rex* episode as another case of dis-integration as the last attempt to mobilize the entire community in the film, "Though the film moves back to town, the return home is really a return to the death of town, community, and relatedness." Of course, the scene that follows, in the fog, confirms Burke's sad reading of the film, notwithstanding the many comic situations and the fact that *Amarcord*, he says " points less to the pessimism of Fellini's earliest movies than to his final films of detachment and resignation."

THE FUNCTION OF MUSIC IN *AMARCORD*

I have adopted Liliana Betti's division of *Amarcord* into 137 scenes (see Angelucci-Betti in Bibliography). The scenes described here are only those with music on the soundtrack plus a few scenes which I deem important to the narrative's context. Be advised that Scene 34, "The search for the lost ring in the septic tank of the Conti di Lovignano," described by Betti in her reconstruction of the postproduction script, was never printed.

The musical examples illustrating my descriptions have been printed with the permission of the publisher C.A.M. s.r.l. of Rome. They have been compiled from the following sources:

1. The film itself, examined in two video-cassette versions: Warner Home Video-Pal/Versione italiana and Public Media Home Vision with English subtitles by Gianfranco Angelucci and Peter Bondanella.
2. The Criterion Collection. Laserdisc 1995
3. The Criterion Collection. DVD 1998
4. Bande oginale du film *Amarcord*: Musique de Nino Rota sous la direction de Carlo Savina. CAM SAG LO 9055

TITLES

The music for the titles, hence referred to as "Amarcord," functions in this film like an operatic *Ouverture*. It does, in fact, immediately set the tone of the show: jovial, sentimental, and profoundly human. As the titles roll on the screen, the music seems to underscore the old: "...Once upon a time .." as in a fairy tale. *Amarcord* is, in fact, a tale about memory as the narrative begins in the past, a past, "[which] can be seized only as an image which flashes up at the instant when it can be recognized and is never seen again." Wrote Benjamin,[1] Rota and Fellini selected an opening tune particularly rich in motivic structures meaning "memory."[2] This tune is capable of reflecting the boundaries of Fellini's

---

[1] Benjamin, Walter. *Illuminations. Essays and Reflections*. Edited and with an Introduction by Hannah Arendt (New York: Schocken Books, 1969): 255.
[2] Two documentary films entitled *Zwischen Kino und Konzert-Der Komponist Nino Rota* (1993), directed by Vassili Silovic (81/2. The Criterion Collection, 2001), and Mario Monicelli's *Un amico magico: il Maestro Nino Rota* (Istituto Luce, 1999), show a film clip of Fellini and Rota at work, selecting musical themes for *Amarcord*. After various unsuccessful trials, Rota finally plays at the piano the title theme as we know it, much to Fellini's joy. Fellini declares, "With this theme we can do the entire film!" Whether the two artists were playing for the camera or not is irrelevant

"enclave," a thematic motif "that takes some rather hair-raising turns before ending up harmonically where it started."[3] The melodic typology of this opening theme corresponds pretty much to the 19th century's concept of the so-called feminine musical theme, a lyrically rich legato, descending line, embodying a specific disposition. Such a way of wrapping the opening theme puts indeed the film's characters and the viewer in a collectively nostalgic mood.

SCENES 1 & 2
Outskirts of Town--Exterior--Daytime--Spring.

Houses, backyards, sheets hanging to dry in the sun. Calm breeze. Puffballs filling the air, which the natives call *Le manine di Primavera* (Spring's early signs).

Titta's House--Exterior--Daytime--Spring.

Titta's backyard. Gina (the housekeeper) and Grandfather look at the puffballs with childish marvel.

The opening two scenes are characterized by the sound of bells. From the first to the last scene in the film we hear bells "telling" what the town's mood of the moment is going to be, from sunrise to sunset, from birth to death. It is the sound of that "medieval enclosure" Fellini often talks about in *Amarcord*.[4] From the volume of the bells' ringing we know immediately that we are in a small town, that people are listening attentively. In Fascist Italy the bells served to punctuate various rituals and events as described by Emilio Gentile: "In 1932

---

in this instance, because such was in reality, their working method. See also "Roma, 11 febbraio 1964. Lavorare con Federico...Conversazione con Nino Rota di Gideon Bachman." A cura di Roberto Calabretto in Veniero Rizzardi (a cura) *L'undicesima Musa: Nino Rota e i suoi media* (Roma: Rai-Eri, 2001): 181-198.
[3] Brown, Royal S. *Overtones and Undertones* (Berkeley, CA: University of California Press, 1994): 220.
[4] Fellini, Federico. "Amarcord: The Fascism within Us." In Angelucci, Gianfranco and Liliana Betti. *Il film "Amarcord" di Federico Fellini* (Bologna: Cappelli, 1974): 24-25.

[Party Secretary] Achille Starace sought to make the symbolic presence of the party more resonant by decreeing -- once again in imitation of the Catholic tradition -- that every *Casa del Fascio* (party headquarters) should include a 'lictorial tower with bells,' which would be rung on party occasions. With its bells, 'both mystical and popular,' the party was invoking a centuries-old civic and religious tradition, thus making its 'original and ever more lively form of religion' more expressive."[5] Thanks to Fellini, the Adriatic town of Rimini has become a capital of the collective imagination like the Rome of Rossellini and Pasolini, the New York of Scorsese and Woody Allen, the Paris of Clair and Truffaut, and ultimately the London of Hitchcock.[6] In sum, as Attali wrote about bells, "It is the sound by which society can be judged."[7] In film history, there are innumerable examples of the use of church bells. Sergej Eisenstein was a master at it, definitely influenced by the music of Prokofiev who in turn was influenced by that of Mussorgsky. In more recent times, a good example can be found in Ingmar Bergman's *Persona* (1967) in which "church bells created the impression of a small slumbering village."[8]

French film music theorist Michel Chion calls such use of bells *passive off-screen sound* whose principal components he classifies as *territory sound* and *elements of auditory setting*, thus representing "an extension of the sound environment being designated for the degree of openness and breadth of the concrete space suggested by sounds, beyond the borders of the visual field, and also within the visual field around the characters."[9]

---

[5] Gentile, Emilio. *The Sacralization of Politics in Fascist Italy*, transl. by Keith Botsford (Cambridge, MA: Harvard University Press, 1996): 69.
[6] Brunetta, Giampiero. *Cent'anni di cinema italiano*. Vol. 2 (Bari: Editori Laterza, 1998): 55.
[7] Attali, Jacques. *Noise* (Minneapolis: The University of Minnesota Press, 1992, 4th): 3.
[8] Chion, Michel. *Audio-Vision* (New York: Columbia University Press, 1994): 86.
[9] Chion, Michel. *Op. Cit.*: 87.

SCENE 8

Main Street (*Corso*)--Barbershop--Interior--Evening--Spring.

      This music is heard at the opening of the scene as the camera focuses on the barbershop. Inside the shop, patrons, the barber, and *La Gradisca*, a hairdresser, chat. One patron asks the barber, "What is the band going to play tonight?" and the barber, quickly disposing of the razor and grabbing his flute, replies, "A new composition of mine which sounds like this," and he plays the theme already heard at the beginning of the scene. *La Gradisca*, in the meantime, wiggles her *derrière* to the rhythm of the tune much to the patrons' amusement. The brief episode is a remarkable example of diegetic -- non-diegetic dialectic, as the barber plays diegetically to an unseen (non-diegetic) accompaniment. The episode is also significant, showing the role that song and dance will assume throughout the film: not as mere additional stimulus, like in a farce, but as an integral part of the picture.[10]

---

[10] Eisler, Hanns and Theodor W.Adorno. *Composing for the Films*. New Introduction by Graham McCann (London: The Athelon Press, 1994): 123.

SCENE 9

La fogaraccia. Main Street-Main Square --Exterior--Evening--Spring

People busy gathering toward Main Square. Cantarel, the blind accordionist, arrives placing himself on a short pylon against a wall. Off camera he begins to play *Siboney*.[11] Although the viewer does not see Cantarel actually playing, it is obvious that his music is part of the diegesis. Bells ringing, explosions of firecrackers, and street noises underscore this scene which culminates in the arrival of a procession holding high a large, grotesque puppet representing the old witch of Winter, the allegoric female past the age of reproduction. The puppet is eventually burned on a huge pile of useless objects and broken furniture people are willing to "sacrifice" in a great bonfire celebrating the passing of Winter and the arrival of Spring. The procession is preceded by the *banda comunale* (Community Band) which, led by the barber and

---

[11] *Siboney*. Words and music by Cuban composer Ernesto Lecuona (1896-1963). This very popular song, composed in 1929, nostalgically evokes *Siboney*, a place in Havana, Cuba. One can see a significance in Rota's repeated use of this song: nostalgia for a small, far away place. For Lecuona, busy writing for musicals, films, and radio in New York City, it was *Siboney*. For Fellini and Rota and all the "Amarcordians," including the viewers, it was a place far away in memory.

his flute, plays *La fogaraccia* (The Great Bonfire) a theme sampled before by the barber in his shop.[1]

This undisciplined bunch plays in a rather vulgar fashion, stepping back and forth and swinging their instruments left and right toward the people watching them. The episode concludes with the fire burning high and the people holding hands, performing a sort of round dance which looks like a combination of Brueghel's *Carnival's Quarrel with Lent* and Fellini's grand final scene from *Otto e mezzo*. It is not surprising that ritual ceremonies, whose purpose ultimately is to bond individuals to a sense of common purpose, find music to be essential for accomplishing such a task.

This piece, one of the most extensive in the soundtrack, is reminiscent of Stravinsky's *L'Histoire du Soldat*, the *Royal March* in particular: The opening quintuplet in Stravinsky denotes the oddity of the march's rhythmic structure, while in Rota the opening five notes emphasize the out-of-steps and out-of-tune stance of the musicians on screen.

---

[1] For the psychology of burning rituals, see Gaston Bachelard's *La Psychanalyse du feu* (Paris, 1949) and Jacob A. Arlow. "Pyromania and the Primal Scene: A Psychoanalytic Comment on the Works of Yukio Mishima," *Psychoanalitic Quarterly* 47 (1978): 24-51.

SCENE 11

Main Street-Main Square--Exterior--Night--Spring

The feast is ended. People gradually head for their homes while Cantarel plays for the first time "his" very nostalgic tune.[13] In *Amarcord*, Cantarel's accordion becomes a symbolic presence emanating some redeeming qualities similar to *Gelsomina*'s trumpet in *La Strada*.[14]

SCENE 15

Senior High classroom--Interior--Daytime--Spring

A teacher lectures on Medieval history. His only concern, however, seems to be the ashes of his cigarette which he skillfully manages to keep intact. Upon Titta's wrong answer regarding a datum, he explodes in a fit of rage, screaming, "You are driving me mad, YOU ARE DRIVING ME MAD!" The utterance is underscored by a sinuous little motif played on an electric piano. This tune was originally intended to accompany, in some form, the Mad Uncle episode, Scene 74, which was ultimately printed with no musical soundtrack.

---

[13] The figure of the blind musician playing at night goes back to Novalis and the early German romantics who sought the Truth in the blindness of night. A similar character was also represented in Baudelaire's *Le Vieux Saltimbanque*, Manet's *The Old Musician*, and Daumier's *Saltimbanque Playing a Drum* among others.

[14] Gorbman, Claudia. "Music as Salvation: Notes on Fellini and Rota." *Film Quarterly* 28 No. 3 (1974-75): 17-25.

SCENE 23

Boys' Restroom--Interior--Daytime--Spring

Titta, Ovo, and Ciccio furtively share a cigarette by an open window through which one distinctly hears a woman singing *Stormy Weather*. We shall hear this song on other occasions during the film, always in association with the characters' feeling of guilt, fear and/or outburst of rage . Rota's very clever, psychological use of this motif can be interpreted as symbolic for prohibition and as applying the adjective "stormy" to episodes in which the protagonists' temper provokes "stormy" reactions: during the math lesson when the urination prank is played on one of the students and in Scene 28.[15]

SCENE 28

Titta's House--Kitchen Table--Interior--Daytime--Spring

This is a most picturesque episode in which the entire household has gathered around the kitchen table for dinner (one o'clock *pranzo* in Italy). Waiting for the food to be served is characterized by waiting for another "dish" to be served: the *Giornale Radio*.[16] In Italy the one o'clock news was, for decades, preceded by an intermittent nightingale's sweet call as a station and identification signal just as it is heard on the film's soundtrack. It was a ritual that has accompanied, and still does today, though somewhat replaced by television news, the *pranzo* of millions of Italians. The radio bird call in *Amarcord*, therefore, replaces the church bells, as the town splits into hundreds of tiny enclaves, the families, a microcosm in which past values coexist with symbols of modernity

---

[15] This song was composed by Harold Arlen (1905-1986) in 1933 for Ethel Waters as part of a set of scenes presented at the Cotton Club in Harlem during the Prohibition Era. The "Stormy Weather Show," as it came to be called, was one of the most successful ever staged at the Cotton Club. See Haskins, Jim. *The Cotton Club* (New York: Hippocrene Books, 1994): 87. Later, the song, became Lena Horne's signature. When the picture *Stormy Weather* was made in 1943, Lena Horne was its star.

[16] In June 1930, the Italian State Radio (E.I.A.R.) began to broadcast regularly an official news program. In 1935, with the installation of powerful facilities in Rome, the *Giornale Radio* was presented in two very popular editions: at one o'clock and one-fifty. See Monteleone, Franco. *Storia della radio e della televisione in Italia* (Venezia: Marsilio, 1992): 89.

and wellbeing. The bird call is a phantom sound since there is no radio receiver in sight in the kitchen. However, when Grandfather moves to the adjacent formal dining room for his ritual exercise in flatulence, a furniture-like radio receiver is shown as part of the decor of a small land owner-builder's house such as Aurelio's.

During the *pranzo* scene, Aurelio's outburst of rage directed against Titta's behavior and his perennial squabbles with Miranda, is punctuated by the same female voice heard before singing *Stormy Weather*.

SCENE 32

Lo struscio (the strolling) on Main Street--Shopping--Exterior--Evening-Spring

[A]

[B]

[C]

[D]

The evening promenade on the *Corso* where everybody goes to see and be seen. This episode is characterized by a combination of motifs. Rota opens the sequence with "Amarcord" played with a bouncy Fox-Trot flair, symbolizing the affair's enjoyable pace. [A] The "Amarcord" motif is heard every time the camera focuses on the townspeople; otherwise Rota presents a variety of motifs, each symbolizing "outside" influences and values. Following "Amarcord," we hear *Quel motivetto che mi piace tanto.* [B][17] followed by a heavy swing instrumental rendition of *Stormy Weather* [C] as the camera passes by the *Cinema Fulgor,* the

---

[17] This very popular for-trot, written by Dan Caslar and Michele Galdieri in 1932, was made famous by Tecla Scarano in the musical *Strade* (Streets). See Borgna, Gianni. *Storia della canzone italiana* (Milano: Mondadori, 1992): 134.

place where American movies are shown. The theatre signifies guilt for escaping from reality, i.e. Fascism, the Catholic Church, the burden of provincial family life. We return briefly to *Quel motivetto* and "Amarcord," followed by loud strains of *La cucaracha*. [D][18] This tune underscores the passage of a carriage revealing the town's *nuova quindicina*, the newly arrived prostitutes available at the local brothel for the next two weeks. The scene brings to mind Kirchner's city paintings in which the artist tends to focus on the prostitute, whose smart appearance, while flirting with "respectability," is a symbol of bourgeois hypocrisy and an affirmation of bourgeois consumption.[19] Rota, on the other hand, performs here a magnificent psychological and even physiological portrait of the place by juxtaposing "Amarcord" played as a jovial Fox-Trot first and later by an "angelic" glockenspiel, to *Stormy Weather* executed on a raucous saxophone symbolizing some kind of cinematic "fallen woman" music,[20] and also to *Quel motivetto*, a good all Italian (despite its jazzy mood) radio song. Finally, the euphoric, exotic, festive Mexican song *La cucaracha* is heard again while the people (males, females, and children) look at the displayed "merchandise" with signs of approval, suspicion, desire, and envy as if they were at a grand carnival they so much enjoyed in Carmen Miranda's movies.

Lo struscio constitutes the longest continuous music sequence in the film. Remarkable is the presence of quoted popular songs which, aside from bringing back 1930's memories, appear to promote the utopia of the small town in a clear, uncomplicated way.[21]

Incidentally, these songs come, directly or not, from movies and shows dealing with street scenes. Rota wished, perhaps, to pay homage to the Parisian

---

[18] This Mexican folk tune was published in 1934 in a transcription made by Domenico Savino. It reached enormous popularity in a RKO two-reeler Technicolor entitled *La cucaracha* (1933). See Barrios, Richard. *A Song in the Dark: The Birth of the Musical Film* (New York: Oxford University Press, 1995): 427.
[19] Quoted in Butler, Christopher. *Early Modernism* (Oxford: Oxford University Press, 1994): 190.
[20] On the concept of music and female sexuality in cinema see Kalinak, Kathryn. *Settling the Score: Music in the Classical Hollywood Film* (Madison: The University of Wisconsin Press, 1992).
[21] Flinn, Caryl. *Strains of Utopia: Gender, Nostalgia and Hollywood Film Music* (Princeton, NJ: Princeton University, 1992): 111.

folklore of Cocteau and Auric and, perhaps ,even the Debussy of *Gigues* (based on Verlaine's *Streets*).

SCENE 46
Cinema Fulgor--Balcony--Interior--Daytime--Spring

The music, a syncopated, almost cartoonish version of "Amarcord," follows Titta as he leaps from seat to seat until he finds a place next to *La Gradisca* where he makes his move by crawling his hand under the woman's dress. *La Gradisca* sits in a trance-like state watching Gary Cooper in *Beau Geste*. As she feels Titta's hand on her thigh, she exhales a huge puff of cigarette smoke as in a post-orgasmic state, then, very indifferently asks Titta, "Do you want something?" as the "Amarcord" theme bursts forth in a full orchestral blow, while a much bigger than life close-up of Gary Cooper appears on the screen. Titta feels scorned, and the "Amarcord" theme, sparingly and nostalgically played on a piano brings the scene to a close. The function of the orchestral "tutti," serves to aggrandize *La Gradisca*'s appreciation for Cooper's image, while the tiny fading-out sound of the piano reflects, by contrast, Titta's disappointment and retraction into his "inner time."

SCENE 49
Fascist Parade of April 21st--Railroad Station Plaza--Exterior--Daytime--Spring.

Rome is our point of departure and our reference; it is our symbol, or, if you wish, our myth.
Benito Mussolini, *Passato e avvenire*, in "Il Popolo d'Italia," April 21, 1922

In 1925 Benito Mussolini officially proclaimed April 21 to be the day Rome was founded. The celebration of this event, *Il Natale di Roma,* was interpreted by Fascists as "an initiation rite that opened the way to communion with *Romanitá*. Through this rite, which was animated by a solar willpower, an imperial will, a will to power...the new Italian could make spiritual contact with ancient Rome."[22] In practice, the new national holiday served as a substitute for the abolished May 1st Labor Day celebration.

This is the only overtly political episode in the film. Fascist and anti-Fascist sentiments are placed at the forefront, feelings which have afflicted many of the Italian people during the *ventennio*. For the long episode, Rota used a vast array of Party, patriotic, and military tunes to underscore the people's shifts of sentiment.

PART ONE

We see the community band in military-like attire at the beginning of the ceremony at the railroad station's plaza. Trumpet calls and drum rolls announce the arrival "on time" of the train carrying the *Federale* (Regional Fascist Party Secretary); The band plays the Fascist hymn *Verrá quel di verrá*, then accompanies the *cortège* headed by the *Federale* on a trot-march to a *Bersaglieri* song as had became customary in ceremonies of this kind.[23] Later, during the festivities, the raising of Mussolini's gigantic floral effigy is characterized by a diegetic performance of Giacomo Puccini's *Inno a Roma*,[24] followed by strains of Mendelssohn's *Wedding March* as Ciccio envisions himself marrying Aldina, with *Il Duce*'s flower-effigy celebrating the vows. The episode is Fellini's clever satire of Italian religious and political establishments.

---

[22] Gentile, Emilio. *Op. Cit.*: 78.
[23] The *Bersaglieri* infantry division (ShookTroops), founded by General La Marmora in 1836, was known for its great mobility and precision.
[24] Puccini's innocuous hymn (text by Fausto Salvatori) was composed in 1919 for use in Roman schools. It became a Fascist Youth Party song. Some very popular recordings made in 1938 and 1940 coupled the hymn with *Giovinezza*, the official Fascist Party song. According to the social historian Luisa Passerini, "In the late forties the influence of Fascism was still pervasive in my elementary school: I remember poems and hymns like 'Sun that rises free and joyful/over our hills your horses rule/you will never see anything in the world/greater than Rome, greater than Rome.' [Puccini's *Inno a Roma*]. The teacher instilled in us the cult of Rome, as a supreme place." Passerini, Luisa. *Autobiography of a Generation, Italy, 1968*. Trans. by Lisa Erdberg (Hanover and London: Wesleyan University Press, 1996): 11. Further information on Fascist hymnology can be found in Savona, Virgilio and Michele L. Straniero. *Canti dell'Italia fascista, 1919-1945* (Milano: Garzanti, 1996).

PART TWO

At the end of the festive day, cheers, toasts, and society games are accompanied by non-diegetic strains of *Siboney* played by guitar and accordion. Nostalgia for a far away place? The evening is suddenly shaken by the sound of a scratchy violin playing the *Internationale*.[25] After much searching for the subversive intruder, it is found that the tune is produced by a phonograph hidden in the church bell tower. Fellini purposely shows how the church has become part of the regime's politics. After the phonograph is shot down, a group of fascists sings Giuseppe Blanc's *All'armi, All'armi siam fascisti*[26] in a defiant mood. The episode concludes with the fascists interrogating Aurelio while forcing him to drink castor oil in order to " purge" any lingering socialist ideas out of his mind and... body.

---

[25] The original version of the *Internationale*, text by Eugène Pottier, was set to music by Pierre Dugeyter. It was composed for the choral society, "La Lyre des travailleurs, " of Lilla and performed for the first time in 1889, when the Guesdists and Broussists organized in Paris on June 14, the date of the storming of the Bastille and a national holiday, the founding congress of the new International Workingman's Association, also referred to as the Socialist International or Second International. The song, published in several editions (1894, 1898, 1904), became, in 1917, the official hymn of the Soviet Union until 1944 when it was replaced by Grigori Alexandrov's. The song, translated into all languages, was published in Italy in 1901; See Settimeli, Leoncarlo and Laura Falavolti. *Canti socialisti a comunisti* (Roma: Savelli, 1973): 30 and Lindman, Albert S. *A History of European Socialism* (New Haven: Yale University Press, 1983): 148.

[26] This was an old World War I song composed by Giuseppe Blanc which the Arditi introduced to the Fascist hymnology after several textual changes. See Carrara, Lino. *Canti fascisti* (Pisa: Simoncini, 1923): 10.

SCENE 66

Suite at the Grand Hotel--Interior--Nighttime--Winter.

Throughout this episode, which, according to hearsay, gives Ninola the nickname "La Gradisca," the theme "Amarcord" is heard as a slow waltz played by violins with lush and languid *glissandi* in a rather decadent fashion akin to the nature of the episode and the characters portrayed in it.

Music plays a very important function in this pantomime episode in which the body movements of the Prince, in high military garb like a *miles gloriosus*, and of his *entourage*, reflect the tradition of the Italian *commedia dell'arte*. Ninola makes, in fact, a delightful Colombine, while the Prince and his *aides de camp* might as well be Pierrot and Arlequin (s). They move following the waltz's waves as in a mild stupor, the Prince certainly assisted by the champagne he and his aides have been drinking all along, Ninola by the glamour of the situation. When she finally utters her "famous" line, "*Signor Principe, Gradisca!*" the spell is broken, the grand music and the scene fade-out. The Prince has surely consummated the "offer" Ninola and the town folks had reserved especially for him. In traditional patriarchy, the prince is assumed to hold the position of absolute masculinity; he stands in the public place of the superego. He becomes the exception to the rule that no one can hold this position, and this assumption justifies the fact that other men, subject to the prince, can never hold it.[27] This exquisite pantomime is Fellini's and Rota's spoof on Prince Umberto di Savoia, heir to the Crown of Italy, who enjoyed a reputation with the ladies. He eventually became the King of Italy as Umberto II for only 25 days (May 9-June 2, 1946). According to Rota " Fellini wanted to use *Fascination*, a celebrated waltz-tune by Marchetti to underscore the episode, a song "Fellini insists on using in his films every time a 1930's situation involves a more or less attractive woman. However, at the last moment, *Fascination* could not be used because of failure in reaching a suitable copyright agreement. In the end, the film's opening theme, rhythmically transformed, became the best possible solution."[28]

SCENE 67
Foyer of Grand Hotel--Interior--Daytime--Spring.

The "Amarcord" theme, delicately played by piano and violin in Palm Court style, underscores the town lawyer, a sort of *flâneur,* and self-appointed *historicus* recounting another local legend: The arrival two years prior of a Caliph with his thirty concubines.

---

[27] Quoted in Kramer, Lawrence. *After the Lovedeath: Sexual Violence and the Making of Culture* (Berkeley, CA: University of California Press, 1997): 177-78.
[28] Quoted in De Santi, Pier Marco. *Nino Rota: Le Immagini & la Musica* (Pisa: Giunti, 1992): 107.

SCENE 68

Main entrance of Grand Hotel--Exterior--Daytime--Spring.

As a bus unloads the exotic *entourage*, Rota's music blasts in a parody of Khachaturian's *Sabre Dance*.[29] At the arrival of the Caliph, who addresses everyone in French, the music switches to the song *Abat-jour*.[30]

Some diegetic clarinet music is heard when Biscein, the town liar, shown in the film playing a homemade recorder, recounts his seduction dream with all the Caliph's wives. With his music he, in fact, enchants the odalisques as they were snakes. A finale *à la Sheherazade*, mixing the scene's opening theme with *La fogaraccia*, underscores the burlesque and absurd story Biscein, like an intruder in the pleasure gardens of Haroun Alraschid, is about to tell.

This episode, patterned after classical antiquity in which the "immoderate lust was priapism, which was like drunkenness, the fault of fools and satyrs."[31]

---

[29] The *Sabre Dance* was a celebrated number in the ballet *Gayane* composed by Aram Khachaturian in 1942, an homage to the circus and its people which Fellini and Rota have paid many times.

[30] *Abat-jour* was the title of a song by Ennio Neri for the music of Mario Robianco. It was made famous by Italian chanteuse Anna Fougez in the 1920's in the style of the French *tabarin*. About this popular song Gian Franco Venè wrote: "Poets are always able to spin words to be set to music: an innocent lamp shade (*abat-jour*) could become an indiscreet or discreet, as the case might be, witness to nights of intense lovemaking." *La canzone italiana* 3 (Milano: Fabbri Editori, 1970, 2nd 1982). Translation is mine. Interestingly, after the March on Rome, a parody of this song, entitled *Manganel*, was widely circulated among fascists. The *manganello* was the wooden club used by fascist thugs to impart "discipline." See Savona and Straniero. *Op. Cit*.: 100. I wonder if Fellini and Rota deliberately selected this song for its double meaning.

SCENE 73

Terrace of Grand Hotel--Exterior--Evening--Summer.

A six-piece dance band plays "Amarcord" with a rhythm of beguine while the guests (early summer foreign tourists) dance. The beguine then turns to a rumba (*La cucaracha*).

This dance-musical diegetic episode is interesting as Rota uses two tunes to underscore two different, yet related, psychological states of mind. First of all, "Amarcord" is not a dance tune of the 1930's; it functions, therefore, as a prelude to Lallo's and the other *vitelloni*'s seducing strategies. Upon hearing *La cucaracha* we realize that the seduction has indeed been accomplished, that Lallo, for instance, has, in fact, "scored points" with the German lady he is pursuing. Lallo later reveals to the band leader (the barber) that the woman was so in love that she even requested from him the forbidden pleasures of anal sex. A nostalgic solo piano version of "Amarcord" underscores the lawyer's professorial discourse on Dante and Leopardi addressed to an aging American tourist. The notes of the piano fade into the following scene: *Lo zio matto* (the Mad Uncle), which although originally provided with a theme (see Scene 15), remains musically silent.

SCENE 83

Beach--Exterior--Daytime--Summer.

The Passing of the *Rex*.[32]

The town folks prepare to sail to high sea to watch up close the passing of the *Rex*. The music underscoring this clumsy yet exciting maneuver is a

---

[31] Paglia, Camille. *Sexual Personae* (London & New Haven: Yale University Press, 1990): 254.
[32] The ocean liner *Rex*, pride of the Societá di navigazione Italian and Mussolini's regime, was launched in 1932. She was 249 meters long, 29 meters wide and 13 meters high, weighting 51.062 tons and cruising at 26 knots per hour. The *Rex* held the prestigious "Blue Ribbon" during the years 1933-35. Inactive in the port of Trieste during World War II, and damaged by aerial bombardment, it was finally scrapped.

streamlined version of *La fogaraccia* played alternately by a trumpet and accordion. Once the *cortège* finally takes off we are offered a close-up of a corpulent, unattractive sailor attempting to sing *Santa Lucia*,[33] telling us that the event is a jovial excuse for a huge community outing on the boats as during the old sunny days in the picturesque bay of Naples.

SCENE 92
High sea--Exterior--Night--Summer.

The passing of the *Rex* is one of the most memorable episodes in the film. Away from their "enclaves," the folks, aboard a myriad of little boats, float like tiny islands in a fantasy sea. In the surreal calm of the water, as they await the portentous passing of the mythical ocean liner, they confide to each other their inner thoughts and sentiments. Fellini has created a touching and human collage beautifully underscored by Nino Rota's kaleidoscopic musical ideas assigned to nearly every character in the scene.

In the background, we hear an accordion (Cantarel's) playing strains from *Stramilano*,[34] then we hear Lallo passionately singing fragments from a Rudy Valentino's *Tango-Cancion* with guitar accompaniment. As a quiet evening descends upon the folks during their vigil (the *Rex* is not scheduled to pass until midnight), the theme "Amarcord" is played by solo guitar and then by guitar and accordion thus bringing Cantarel on the scene. He plays diegetically "his" theme, with a heartfelt melancholy accompanied by spasmodic body contortions aimed at anticipating the syncopations of the song's *tempo di beguine*. Cantarel's accordion and "his" theme assume here a co-protagonist role, underscoring *La*

---

[33] This little gem of a song was written by Enrico Cossovich and Teodoro Cottrau in 1848. It is often considered the very first exemplar of Italian popular song. It is interesting to note that in Sweden, this tune is used as a liturgical hymn in honor of St. Lucia.

[34] This song by Ramo and Mascheroni was written in 1937 in praise of Milano's city life, emphasizing the modernity of Mussolini's Italy. The song was successfully revived in 1962. The reader should be reminded that Milano was the subject of a 1929 documentary film by Corrado D'Errico called *Stramilano*, a homage to the cultural movement *Stracittà* (ultra-city) juxtaposed to *Strapaese* (ultra-country), the movement praising the virtues of country life.

Stracittà and *Strapaese* (Progress and Tradition) formed the two basic tenets of Italian Fascism's cultural life.

Gradisca's sentimental monologue about her wishes to find a suitable husband. The same theme, diegetically played by Cantarel, will bring the film to a close at *La Gradisca*'s wedding, thus connecting her wishes to reality.

A terrific drone finally awakens the floating town folks. It is the *Rex* which appears with all its might, as the "Amarcord" theme surges in grand style to create an outstanding point of synchronization between sound and visual events. The episode, having reached its climax, magically fades into the following scene, the Great Fog, which has no music on the soundtrack.

SCENE 99

Terrace of Grand Hotel--Exterior--Daytime--Autumn.

The Grand Hotel is closed for the season. The boys peep through the cracks of the terrace door and fantasize about the glamorous events that have taken place inside the establishment. At the sound of "Amarcord" played by an imaginary dance band, they improvise a dance scene with imaginary, beautiful female partners. Fellini and Rota have created here a surrealistic ballet of figures, fog and shadows.

SCENES 108-110

Cinema Fulgor--Interior--Daytime--Winter.

A film about jungle and wild beasts takes place. The boys, out of boredom, bounce in their front row seats in a sort of masturbatory propulsion at the rhythmical pounding of heavy Freudian drums coming from the soundtrack.[35] Suddenly, though, a voice calls their attention; it is snowing outside, and so they flee the theatre as from a Sartrean claustrophobia toward newfound freedom and openness. The outside scene is underscored by a jazzy version of "Amarcord" played on an accordion.

---

[35] On this concept see "A Congo Song in the Heart of Darkness" in Dijkstra, Bran. *Evil Sisters* (New York: Alfred A. Knopf, 1996): 160.

SCENE 124
Main Street--Main Square--Exterior--Daytime--Winter.

A snowball fight among the boys, grownups and La Gradisca. The music is "Amarcord."

SCENE 129
Town church--Interior--Daytime--Spring.

Miranda's funeral. Don Balosa sings the *De Profundis.*

SCENES 130-133
Town church--Exterior--Daytime--Spring.

Funeral procession. The Community Band, unseen, but obviously part of the procession, plays a dirge tune called *Una lacrima sulla tomba di mia madre*[36] with much dragging and almost comic sloppiness, especially when the *cortége* passes by the *Cinema Fulgor*. Here, a poster advertising a coming attraction, shows Laurel and Hardy as a symbiotic *homo ludens*, almost as a participant, suggesting comic relief by revealing the foolishness of human play or perhaps the ultimate absurdity of life.

SCENE 137
Wedding Picnic in the Country--Exterior--Daytime--Spring.

According to Vladimir Propp, the hero's courtship and marriage are among the most widespread motifs in myth, folktale, and in epic poetry.[37] In *Amarcord*, Gradisca's wedding to Matteo, a *carabiniere* (Royal Guard) from out-

---

[36] A celebrated funeral march composed by Amedeo Vella (1866-1931).
[37] Propp, Vladimir. *Theory and History of Folklore* (Minneapolis: University of Minnesota Press, 1984).

of-town, concludes the film with a festive, yet melancholy Springtime occasion. In the end, Ninola does not find the Gary Cooper of her dreams, but a simple *carabiniere*, though still a man in uniform. Incidentally, the actor playing Matteo (the *carabiniere*) previously appeared in the film as one of the Prince's attendants (see Scene 66); it might seem, according to Fellini, that he may already have somehow entered Gradisca's subconscious. Furthermore when Matteo is called upon to toast his bride, he identifies her with *Italia*, the Motherland to which he has sworn devotion, by emphatically uttering *VIVA L'ITALIA!* Such an exclamation, the title of a Roberto Rossellini film commemorating the centenary of Italian national unity, was considered by Federico Fellini as a possible title of what became the film *Amarcord*. In this final scene, somewhere, a guitarist plays *Siboney*, which is overtaken by Cantarel's accordion. Again, Lecuona's song of longing and hope underscores the Amarcordians's mood. Finally, among toasts and cheers, Cantarel is guided to a chair facing the banquet table. He begins his diegetic performance by playing "Amarcord," and then "his" theme accompanied by more body contortions than usual, a way, perhaps, to make himself more "visible," a behavior not uncommon among blind musicians.

The accordion's melancholy sound and the sight of Cantarel, the only character in the film who never saw *Amarcord*, but felt it, brings the film to a close.[38] It would seem that, with Titta's coming of age and Miranda's funeral, Gradisca's wedding is just another departure.

For Fellini and Rota, the closing scene is a cordial
ARRIVEDERCI AL PROSSIMO FILM!

In fact, after *La dolce vita* and *Otto e mezzo*, Fellini's films became variants of the same story. The characters encounter each other time and time again, thus acknowledging that they belong to the same genealogical and imaginative tree.

---

[38] It should be noted that, in 1974, Rota published a song version of Cantarel's theme entitled *Mia malinconia* (My Melancholy) with verse by another luminary of Italian cinema, Lina Wertmüller.

BIBLIOGRAPHY

Adorno, Theodor W. *Introduction to the Sociology of Music*, trans. E.B. Ashton (New York, Seabury, 1976).

Angelucci, Gianfranco and Liliana Betti. *Il film 'Amarcord' di Federico Fellini* (Bologna: Cappelli, 1974).

Attali, Jacques. *Noise: The Political Economy of Music* (Minneapolis: The University of Minnesota Press, 1992, 4th).

Barrios, Richard. *A Song in the Dark: The Birth of the Musical Film* (New York: Oxford University Press, 1995).

Benjamin, Walter. *Illuminations:Essays and Reflections.* Edited and with an Introduction by Hannah Arendt. Trans. Harry Zohn (New York: Schocken Books, 1969).

Berther, Catherine. *Sociocritique de la musique de film* (Montpellier: Centre d'etudes et de recherches sociocritique, Université Paul-Valery, 1993).

Bondanella, Peter. *The Cinema of Federico Fellini* (Princeton: Princeton University Press, 1992).

---------------------- *Federico Fellini: Essays in Criticism* (New York: Oxford University Press, 1978).

---------------------- and Cristina Degli-Esposti. *Perspectives on Federico Fellini* (New York: G.K. Hall & Cp., 1993)

----------------------"Recent Works on Italian Cinema." *Journal of Modern Italian Studies*, Vol. 1, No. 1, Fall 1995: 101-23.

Borgna, Gianni. *Storia della canzone italiana* (Milano: Mondadori, 1992).

Borin, Fabrizio (a cura). *La filmografia di Nino Rota*. Archivio Nino Rota. Studi I (Firenze: Olschki, 1999).

Brown, Royal S. *Overtones and Undertones: Reading Film Music* (Berkeley: University of California Press, 1994).

Burke, Frank. *Fellini's Films: From Postwar to Postmodernism* (New York: Twayne Publishers, 1996).

Burlingame, Jon. *TV's Biggest Hits* (New York: Schirmer Books, 1996).

Burt, George. *The Art of Film Music* (Boston: Northeastern University Press, 1994).

Carrara, Lino. *Canti fascisti* (Pisa: Simoncini, 1923).

Chandler, Charlotte. *Io, Federico Fellini* (Milano: Mondadori, 1995).

Chion, Michel. *Audio-Vision: Sound on Screen*. Foreword by Walter Murch. Edited and translated by Claudia Gorbman. (New York: Columbia University Press, 1994).

Comuzio, Ermanno and Paolo Vecchi. *138 1/2, i film di Nino Rota* (Reggio Emilia: Assessorato alla Cultura, 1987).

De Santi, Per Marco. *Omaggio a Nino Rota* (Pisa: Assessorato Istituti Culturali, 1981).

------------------------ *La musica di Nino Rota* (Roma: Laterza, 1983).

------------------------ *I disegni di Federico Fellini* (Roma: Laterza, 1989).

------------------------ *Nino Rota: Le Immagini & La Musica* (Firenze: Giunti, 1992).

Dijkstra, Bran. *Evil Sisters* (New York: Alfred A. Knopf, 1996).

Eisler, Hanns and Theodor W. Adorno. *Composing for the Films*. New Introduction by Graham McCann (London: The Athelon Press, 1994).

Ewen, David. *George Gershwin: His Journey to Greatness* (New York: The Ungar Publishing Co., 1976. 2nd 1986).

Fabris, Dinko. *Nino Rota compositore del nostro tempo* (Bari: Orchestra Sinfonica di Bari, 1987).

---------------- "La musica non filmica di Nino Rota: ipotesi di un catalogo," *Musica senza aggettivi*, ed. Agostino Ziino. Vol. 2 (Firenze: Olschki, 1991): 705-55.

----------------and Marco Renzi. *La Musica a Bari* (Bari: Levante Editori, 1993).

Farassino, Alberto and Tatti Sangionetti. *Lux Film: Esthétique et systéme d'un studio italien* (Locarno: Editions du Festival International du Film de Locarno, 1984).

Farassino, Alberto. *Lux Film* (Milano: Il Castoro, 2000).

Federico, Antonella. *Luisa Báccara* (Venezia, Neri Pozza, 1994).

Fellini, Federico and Tonino Guerra. *Amarcord* (Milano: Rizzoli, 1973, 3rd. 1974).

Flinn, Caryl. *Strains of Utopia: Gender, Nostalgia, and Hollywood Film Music* (Princeton: Princeton University Press, 1992).

Frith, Simon. *Performing Rites: On the Value of Popular Music* (Cambridge, MA: Harvard University Press, 1996).

Gentile, Emilio. *Il culto del littorio* (bari: Laterza, 1993). English version by Keith Botsford entitled *The Sacralization of Politics in Fascist Italy* (Cambridge, MA: Harvard University Press, 1996).

Giannetti, Louis D. "Amarcord: The Impure Art of Federico Fellini," *Western Humanities Review* 30 (1976): 153-58.

Gorbman, Claudia. "Music as Salvation: Notes on Fellini and Rota, " *Film Quarterly* 28, No. 3 (1974-75): 17-25.

---------------------- Same reprinted in *Federico Fellini: Essays in Criticism*, ed. Bondanella (New York: Oxford University Press, 1978).

---------------------- *Unheard Melodies: Narrative Film Music* (Bloomington: Indiana University Press, 1987).

Gruen, John. *Menotti: A Biography* (New York: McMillan Publishing Co., Inc. 1978)

Haskins, Jim. *The Cotton Club* (New York: Hippocrene Books, 1994).

Hay, James. *Popular Film Culture in Fascist Italy: The Passing of the Rex* (Bloomington: University of Indiana Press, 1987).

-------------- A selection of this work bearing the title "Grandfather Fascism and Amarcord" has been reprinted in *Perspectives on Federico Fellini*, eds. Peter Bondanella and Cristina Degli-Esposti (New York: G.K. Hall & Co., 1993).

Kalinak, Cathryn. *Settling the Score: Music and the Classical Hollywood Film* (Madison: University of Wisconsin Press, 1992).

Karlin, Fred. *Listening to Movies: The Film Lovers: Guide to Film Music* (New York: Schirmer Books, 1994).

La Morgia, Manlio. "Giovanni Rinaldi: Indicazioni per lo studio di un musicista da 'riscoprire'," *I grandi anniversary del 1960* (Siena: Ticci, 1960): 61-67.

Landy, Marcia. *Fascism in Film: The Italian Commercial Cinema, 1931-1943* (Princeton: Princeton University Press, 1986).

Latorre, Jesus Maria. *Nino Rota: La imagen de la musica* (Barcellona: Montesinos, 1980)

Lee, Andrea. "Really Fellini." *The New Yorker*. Dec. 11, 1995: 94-100.

Lindman, Albert S. *A History of European Socialism* (New Haven: Yale University Press, 1983).

Lombardi, Francesco. " 'Il mago doppio': interrogativi su Nino Rota" *Chigiana*, Vol. XLVII, Nuova Serie No. 22, Anno 1990 (Firenze: Olschki, 1992): 413-21.

------------------------(a cura). *Fra cinema e musica del novecento: il caso Nino Rota dai documenti*. Archivio Nino Rota. Studi II (Firenze: Olschki, 2000).

Marcus, Millicent. "Fellini's Amarcord: Film as Memory." *Quarterly Review of Film Studies* 2 (1977): 418-25.

Marks, Martin M. *Music and the Silent Film: Contexts & Case Studies 1895-1941* (New York: Oxford University Press, 1997).

Miceli, Sergio. *La musica nel film: arte e artigianato* (Fiesole: Discanto/La Nuova Italia, 1982).

------------------ *Morricone, la Musica, il Cinema* (Milano: Mucchi-Ricordi, 1994).

------------------ "Analizzare la music per film: una riproposta della teoria dei livelli. "Rivista Italian di Musicologia, XXIX, 1994: 517-44.

------------------"Storiografia musicale italiana e musica del cinema," *Chigiana*, Vo. XLII, Nuova Serie No. 22, Anno 1990 (Firenze: Olschki, 1992): 201-222.

------------------ *Musica e cinema nella cultura del Novecento* (Firenze: Sansoni, 2000).

Monteleone, Franco. *Storia della radio e della televisione italiana* (Venezia" Marsilio, 1992).

Morelli, Giovanni (a cura). *Storia del candore: Studi in memoria di Nino Rota nel ventesimo della scomparsa*. Archivio Nino Rota III (Firenze: Olschki, 2001).

Mosse, George L. *The Culture of Western Europe* (Boulder: Westview Press, 1988, 3rd.).

Nasta, Dominique. *Meaning in Film: Relevant Structures in Soundtrack and Narrative* (Berne: Lang, 1991).

Naviglio, Giuseppe. *Nino Rota. Il Sacro: Mysterium e Roma Capomunni.* Unpublished thesis. Facoltá di Lettere-Università di Bari, 1993.

Nora, Pierre. "Between Memory and History: Les Lieux de Mémoire!" Representations 26. Spring 1989: 7-25.

Paglia, Camille. *Sexual Personae* (London & New Haven: Yale University Press, 1990).

Palmer, Christopher. *The Composer in Hollywood* (London: Marion Boyars, 1993).

Parshall, Peter F. "Fellini's Thematic Structuring: Patters of Fascism in Amarcord," *Film Criticism* 7, No. 2 (1983): 19-30.

Pasco, Allan H. "The Thematic Structure of Fellini's Amarcord. *1976 Film Studies Annual*. Ed. Ben Lawton (West Lafayette: Purdue University, 1976): 259-71.

Passerini, Luisa. *Autobiography of a Generation: Italy 1968*. Trans. By Lisa Erdberg (Hanover and London: Wesleyan University Press, 1996).

Pinzauti, Leonardo. "A colloquio con Nino Rota." *Nuova Rivista Musicale Italiana* V, 1971: 74-83.

Pizzetti, Bruno. *Ildebrando Pizzetti. Cronologia e Bibliografia* (Parma: La Pilotta, 1980).

Prendergast, Roy M. *Film Music, a Neglected Art* (New York: W.W. Norton & Co., 1977. 2nd 1992).

Raksin, David. "Life with Charlie," *Library of Congress Quarterly* XL/3 (Summer 1983): 234-53.

Riva, Valerio. "La balia in camicia near." *L'Espresso*, Ottobre 7, 1973.

-----------------" Il fascismo dentro di noi" Il film Amarcord (see Angelucci-Betti): 101-107.

----------------"The Fascism within us: Interview with Valerio Riva" in *Federico Fellini: Essays in Criticism* (see Bondanella): 20-26.

Rizzardi, Veniero (a cura). *L'Undicesima Musa: Nino Rota e i suoi media* (Roma: Rai-Eri, 2001).

Rosen, Philip. "Adorno and Film Music: Theoretical Notes on Composing for the films." *Yale French Studies* 60 (1980): 174-81.

Rosza, Milkós. Double Life: *The Autobiography of Miklós Rosza* (New York: Hippocrene Books, 1983).

Rota-Rinaldi, Ernesta. *Mio padre e storia di Nino*. A cura di Francesco Lombardi (Comune di Reiiolo: Reggiolo, 1999).

Savona, Virgilio A. and Michele L. Straniero. *Canti dell'Italia fascista, 1919-1945* (Milano: Garzanti, 1979).

Settimeli, Leoncarlo and Laura Falavolti. *Canti socialisti e comunisti* (Roma: Savelli, 1973).

Simon, John. "The Other Rota," *The New Criterion*, September 2000: 53-59.

Tambling, Jeremy. *Opera, Ideology and Film* (Manchester: Manchester University, 1987).

Tassone, Aldo. "From Romagna to Roma: The Voyage of a Visionary Chronicler (Roma and Amarcord) in *Federico Fellini: Essays in Criticism* (see Bondanella): 261-288.

Vene`, Gian Franco. *La canzone italiana*. No. 3 (Milano: Fabbri Editori, 1970, 2nd 1982).

Verdone, Mario. *Federico Fellini* (Milano: Il Castoro, 1994).

Verginelli, Vinci and Nino Rota. *Bibliotheca Hermetica. Catalogo alquanto ragionato della Raccolta Verginelli-Rota di Antichi Testi Ermetici dei secoli XV-XVIII* (Firenze: Nardini Editore, 1986).

INDEX OF NAMES

A

Adorni, Diana, 31
Adorno, Theodor W., II, 55, 75, 76
Alfano, Franco, VII
Alexandrov, Grigori, 65
Allegret, Marc, 19
Allen, Woody, 54
Alrashid, Haroun, 68
Arlen, Harold, 59
Arlow, Jacob A., 57
Andersen, Hans Christian, 5
Anton, Edoardo, 21
Anfossi, Giovanni Maria, 4
Angelucci, Gianfranco, 32, 51, 53, 75
Arendt, Hannah, 52, 75
Augias, Corrado, 42
Auric, George, 63
Attali, Jacques, II, 54, 75

B

Baccàra, Luisa, 4
Bachman, Gideon, 53
Bachelard, Gaston, 57
Barber, Samuel, 6
Barrios, Richard, 62, 75
Barthes, Roland, II
Bartolucci, Bernardo, 43
Bas, Giulio, 4
Baudelaire, Charles, II, 3, 58
Beluzzi, Maria Antonietta, 31
Benedetti Michelangeli, Arturo, 4
Benjamin, Walter, II, 52, 75
Bennati, Giuseppe, 21
Bergman, Ingmar, 54
Berlin, Irving, 6
Berthet, Catherine, 75
Betti, Liliana, 32, 51, 53
Bianchi, Giorgio, 20, 21, 23
Bianchi, Renzo, 32
Blanc, Giuseppe, 65

Bondanella, Peter, IX, 32, 44, 45, 46, 51, 75, 77, 80
Bondanella Conaway, Julia, 33
Bondarchuk, Sergej Fedorovich, 24
Borgna, Gianni, 61, 75
Borin, Fabrizio, 75
Botsford, Keith, 41, 77
Brahms, Johannes, 6
Brancia, Armando, 31
Brembilla, Ferruccio, 31
Brown, Royal S., 53, 75
Brueghel, Pieter, II, 35, 57
Brunetta, Giampiero, 54
Berlingame, Jon, 75
Burke, Frank, 47, 48, 49, 50, 75
Burt, George, 75
Butler, Christopher, 62

C

Calabretto, Roberto, 53
Calvino, Italo, VIII
Carbonari, David, 20
Carbonatto, Lidia, 4
Carcano, Gianfilippo, 31
Carrara, Lino, 65, 76
Casadio, Aglauco, 22
Casella, Alfredo, 5, 6
Caslar, Dan, 61
Cass, Henry, 11
Castellani, Renato, 9, 11
Castelnuovo-Tedesco, Mario, 5
Chaplin, Charles, 29
Chandler, Charlotte, 76
Chieco, Franco, 9
Chihara, Paul, IX
Chion, Michel, 54, 76
Chopin, Frederick, 4, 5
Cianciulli, Michele, 6
Clair, René, 54
Clement, René, 22

Clerici, Fabrizio, 17
Cocteau, Jean, 63
Coletti, Duilio, 20, 21, 22, 23
Colman, Ronald, 43
Colleoni, Bartolomeo, 40
Comencini, Luigi, 21
Comuzio, Ermanno, 5, 76
Cooper, Gary, 40, 46, 63, 73
Copland, Aaron,I, 6
Coppola, Carmine, 12
Coppola, Francis Ford, VII, 12, 24, 25, 29
Cossovich, Enrico, 70
Cottrau, Teodoro, 70

D

D'Amico, Fedele, 8, 9
D'Amico Cecchi, Suso, 11
D'Annunzio, Gabriele, 4, 40
Dallapiccola, Luigi, 3, 7
Daumier, Honorè, 58
Debussy, Claude, 4, 63
De Falla, Manuel, 5
De Felice, Lionello, 20
De Felice, Fernado, 31
De Filippo Eduardo, 9, 12, 19, 22, 24, 29
De Lauretis, Dino, 12
Degli-Esposti, Cristina, 77
D'Errico, Corrado, 70
Delachi, Paolo, 4
De Santi, Pier Marco, 67, 76
De Sica, Vittorio, 43
di Falco, Marcello, 31
Dijkstra, Bran, 71, 76
Dmytryk, Edward, 23
Donizetti, Gaetano, 3
Dugeyter, Pierre, 65

E

Eisenstein, Sergej, I, 54
Eisler, Hanns, 55, 76
Emmer, Luciano, 22
Erdberg, Lisa, 64, 79

Eusepi, Carmela, 31
Ewen, David, 76

F

Faà di Bruno, Antonino, 31
Fabris, Dinko, VIII, 5
Falavolti, Laura, 65, 80
Farassino, Alberto, 9, 76
Federici, Antonella, 4, 77
Flinn, Caryl, 62, 77
Foss, Lukas, 6
Fougez, Anna, 68
Fracci, Carla, 30
Francisci, Pietro, 19
Frith, Simon, VI, 77

G

Galdieri, Michele, 61
Gambini, Donatella, 31
Gatti, Guido Maggiolino, 8, 9
Gatti Aldrovanti, Clelia, 10
Gavazzeni, Gianandrea, 8
Gentile, Emilio, 41, 54, 64, 77
Gershwin, George, 5, 6
Gervasio, Raffaele, VII
Giannelli, Franco, VIII
Giannetti, Louis, D., 36, 37, 39, 77
Giannini, Ettore, VII
Giordano, Umberto, 9
Girolami, Marino, 19, 20
Giulini, Carlo Maria, 10
Godard, Jean-Kuc, 36, 39
Gorbman, Claudia, 58, 76, 77
Gramsci, Antonio, VII
Griffith, Charles, 29
Gruen, John, 6, 77
Guerra, Tonino, 32, 36, 77
Guillermin, John, 25

H

Hamilton, Guy, 23
Harvey, Anthony, 25

Haskins, Jim, 59, 77
Hay, James, 7, 42, 43, 45, 77
Heine, Heinrich, 3
Hitchcock, Alfred, 54
Horne, Lena, 59
Ianigro, Giuseppe, 31
Ingrassia, Ciccio, 31

J

Jacques, Christian, 22

K

Khachaturian, Aram, 68
Kalinak, Kathryn, 62, 77
Karlin, Fred, 78
Kirchner, Ernst Ludwig, 62
Koechlin, Charles, 5
Kramer, Lawrence, 67
Kurohara, Akira, 25

L

Labiche, Eugene, 9
Landy, Marcia, IX, 7, 77
La Marmora, Alfonso, 64
Latorre, Jesus Maria, 6, 78
Lawton, Ben, 35, 79
Lecuona, Ernesto, 56, 73
Lee, Andrea, 29, 78
Lenzi, Bruno, 31
Lindman, Albert S., 65, 78
Liszt, Franz, 5
Lombardi, Francesco, 4, 10, 78, 80
Lubin, Arthur, 21

M

Maggio, Pupella, 31
Magno, Francesco, 31
Mainardi Colleoni, Ada, 40
Mainardi, Enrico, 40
Malipiero, Gia Francesco, VIII, 7
Mandyczewski, Eusebius, 6
Manet, Edouard, II, 58

Majano, Anton Giulio, 20
Marchetti, F. D., 67
Marks, Martin M., 29, 78
Marcus, Millicent, 38, 39, 46, 78
Marrocco, Gianfranco, 31
Martucci, Giuseppe, 4
Mascagni, Pietro, VII, 9
Mascheroni, Vittorio, 70
Maselli, Francesco, 31
Masina, Giulietta, 44
Matarazzo, Raffaele, 7, 8, 20
Materassi, Sandro, 7
Mather, Marshall, II
McCann, Graham, 55
Mendelssohn, Felix, 64
Menotti, Gian Carlo, 6
Metz, Vittorio, 6
Miceli, Sergio, 78
Miranda, Carmen, 62
Mishima, Yukio, 57
Misul, Mauro, 31
Monicelli, Mario, 21, 22, 25, 52
Monteleone, Franco, 59, 78
Mora, Carla, 31
Morelli, Giovanni, 78
Morricone, Ennio, VII, 12
Mosse, George L., 79
Mozart, Wolfgang Amadeus, 5
Moussorsky, Modest, 54
Murch, Walter, 76
Mussolini, Benito, VII, VIII, 7, 30, 43, 35, 38, 40, 41, 45, 63, 64, 70

N

Nasta, Dominique, 79
Naviglio, Giuseppe, 79
Neri, Ennio, 7, 68
Noël, Magali, 31
Nora, Pierre, 79
Novalis (Friedrich Leopold von Hardenberg), 58

O

Ombra, Gennaro, 31

Orefice, Giacomo, 4
Orfei, Nandino, 31

P

Paganini, Niccoló, 6
Paglia, Camille, 69, 79
Palmer, Christopher, 79
Paolella, Domenico, 19
Paradisi, Giulio, 25
Parshall, Peter F., 39, 41, 79
Pasco, Allan H., 35, 36, 79
Pasolini, Pier Paolo, 43
Passerini, Luisa, 64, 79
Patruno, Lino, 31
Pellegrini, Gluaco, 20
Perlasca, Giovanni, 4
Pertica, Domenico, 31
Petri, Elio, 23
Pinzauti, Leonardo, 79
Pizzetti, Bruno, 40, 79
Pizzetti, Ildebrando, 5, 7, 40
Pool, Jeannie, IX
Porter, Cole, 6
Pottier, Eugène, 65
Prendergast, Roy M., 79
Proietti, Stefano, 31
Prokofiev, Sergej, I, 54
Propp, Vladimir, 72
Proust, Marcel, II, VI
Puccini, Giacomo, VII, 64

R

Raskin, David, 29, 79
Ramo, Enzo, 70
Ravel, Maurice, 5
Reiner, Fritz, 6
Renzi, Marco, 8, 76
Rinaldi, Giovanni, 4, 6
Riva, Valerio, 32, 79, 80
Rizzardi, Veniero, 53, 80
Robianco, Mario, 68
Rorem, Ned, 6
Rosen, Philip, 80

Rossellini, Roberto, 54
Rossen, Robert, 21
Rossi, Franco, 21
Rossi, Luigi, 31
Rózsa, Miklós, 80
Rota-Rinaldi, Ernesta, 4, 5, 13, 80
Rota, Anna Maria, 4
Rota, Nina (Marina), VIII
Rota, Titina, 10

S

Sanguinetti, Tatti, 9, 76
Savina, Carlo, 51
Savino, Domenico, 62
Savona, Virgilio A., 64, 68, 80
Scagnetti, Bruno, 31
Scalero, Rosario, 6
Scarano, Tecla, 61
Scardicchio, Nicola, VIII, 5
Scelsi, Giacinto, 3
Sciannameo, Luciana, IX
Sciannameo, Louise, IX
Schumann, Robert, 4
Scola, Ettore, 43
Scorsese, Martin, 54
Scriabin, Alexander, 4
Settimeli, Leonardo, 65, 80
Sgambati, Giovanni, 4
Shore, Howard, I
Siciliano, Enzo, 32
Signoretti, Fausto, 31
Silovic, Vassili, 52
Simon, John, 29, 80
Sivori, Camillo, 6
Soldati, Mario, 19, 20, 22
Sordi, Alberto, 11
Spaccatini, Antonio, 31
Stagni, Fides, 31
Straniero, Michele L., 64, 68, 80
Strauss, Richard, II
Stravinsky, Igor, II, 5, 57
Strehler, Giorgio, 9

T

Tambling, Jeremy, 80
Tanzilli, Josiane, 31
Tassone, Aldo, 33, 34, 37, 80
Tofano, Sergio, 7
Thomson, Virgil, I
Toscanini, Arturo, 6, 40
Trieste, Leopoldo, 21
Troell, Jan, 25
Truffaut, François, 54

U

Umberto di Savoia, 35, 67

V

Valentino, Rodolfo, 70
Vecchi, Paolo, 5, 76
Vella, Amedeo, 72
Venè, Gian Franco, 68, 80
Verdone, Mario, 80
Verginelli, Vinci, 13, 80
Verlaine, Paul, 63
Verneuil, Henry, 2
Vidor, King, 22
Villella, Armando, 31
Visconti, Luchino, 11, 21, 23, 29
Vitali, Alvaro, 31
Vittorio Emanuele III, 35
Vona Francesco, 31
Vorhaus, Bernard, 19

W

Waters, Ethel, 59
Weill, Kurt, II
Wertmüller, Lina, 11, 24, 29, 41, 43, 45, 73
Wilhelmj, August, 6

Z

Zampa, Luigi, 19
Zanin, Bruno, 31
Zarlino, Gioseffo, II, 6
Zeffirelli, Franco, 11, 24, 29
Ziino, Agostino, 76
Zohn, Harry, 75

APPENDIX

Campane a sera

Nino Rota

Campane a festa

Nino Rota

www.ingramcontent.com/pod-product-compliance
Lightning Source LLC
Chambersburg PA
CBHW030118010526
44116CB00005B/304